You Can Never Get Enough of What You Don't Need

The Quest for Contentment

Mary Ellen Edmunds

DESERET BOOK

Salt Lake City, Utah

For Mary Jane

Library of Congress Cataloging-in-Publication Data

Edmunds, Mary Ellen
    You can never get enough of what you don't need : the quest for contentment / Mary Ellen Edmunds.
        p.   cm.
    Includes bibliographical references and index.
    ISBN 1-59038-383-4 (pbk.)
    1. Contentment—Religious aspects—Christianity. 2. Church of Jesus Christ of Latter-day Saints—Doctrines. 3. Mormon Church—Doctrines. I. Title.
    BV4647.C7E36 2005
    241'.68—dc22
                                                                    2004026434

Printed in the United States of America   72076
Publishers Printing, Salt Lake City, UT

10   9   8   7   6   5   4   3   2

Contents

Preface

This is not a novel. If you thought you were buying a novel, I'm sorry. I hope you'll read the book anyway.

It has a long title, doesn't it? Remember when most books had short titles? *Moby Dick; Black Beauty; Giant.* Now titles seem long, so you don't know what to call the book when you're telling someone else they ought to read it. "It's that one with the long, long title," you might say. "Something about *enough.* Something about *contentment.*"

Would you believe me if I told you this book has helped me? It's true. I've learned and been reminded of many important things while I've been searching, pondering, praying, and writing. These things have been on my mind for more years than I can remember. But I'm not sure when I first realized that not every day or season of my life could be one of contentment unless I worked at it.

You'll notice that some chapters have ideas for what you might consider before you start to read. Some of the chapters have ideas for a family home evening, or a family council, or a get-together with other loved ones or friends (or even people you don't know). There might be a suggestion for a "field trip" or some other activity. Please remember: These suggestions are optional! Use them if they help you.

I decided to include an appendix with books and articles you might find interesting if you want to search more deeply into the topic of contentment. Maybe *you* can write the sequel!

I give sincere thanks to *all* my family and friends who have helped me so much. This includes those who responded to questions I sent recently as well as those who have been studying and sharing with me for a long, long time. Your thank-you note is in the mail! Ha ha.

As I've thought about those who have helped me through the years, I wish to mention Dr. James O. Mason and President Marion G. Romney in particular. Their influence in my life and on my view of the world and individuals is profound.

I thank my friend Cynthia for sharing her poem "Morning Flowers," which she wrote while serving as a missionary in Tainah, Taiwan.

I give a tender thank-you to my four brothers and other family members for the experience on a beautiful

Sunday evening when I was nearing the deadline for finishing this book and needed their help.

I have prayed earnestly for help in preparing this little book, and it is my hope that as you read you won't be annoyed or uncomfortable.

I'm so grateful for Jana Erickson, Emily Watts, Sheryl Smith, and all the rest of the talented, kind team at Deseret Book. Thanks for the opportunity and the encouragement.

In the spirit of what I have hoped to share, I'll be donating to the Church's fast offering funds from the sales of this book. Thanks for helping.

Contentment

The home is on 1200 North, near 300 West. It's a small home with a beautiful yard. Everything looks neat and orderly. There are lots of trees for shade, and many flowers, bushes, and lawn ornaments. It's obvious that someone has gone to a great deal of effort to make things beautiful and pleasant.

What catches my attention when I drive by in the summer at different times of day is how often I see the older gentleman sitting in a chair in the shade of one of the trees reading a book. He looks content.

And, in a way, so does his yard. Sometimes, when I see a place like that, it makes me happy to think that the earth and magic seeds have been helped to accomplish their miracles. It must be a joy for creations to be allowed their full expression. That may be a key to contentment for all living things.

A nineteenth-century poet, W. H. Davies, wrote a poem that to me expresses so well the feeling of contentment:

> Under this tree, where light and shade
> Speckle the grass like a Thrush's breast,
> Here in this green and quiet place
> I give myself to peace and rest.
> The peace of my contented mind,
> That is to me a wealth untold
> When the Moon has no more silver left,
> And the Sun's at the end of his gold.

Aren't those beautiful words? "I give myself to peace and rest." Let them in!

What comes to your mind when you think of the word *contentment?* Perhaps you'll think of a specific experience. When was it? Where were you? What was happening? Does the memory bring back some of the feelings? I'm convinced that contentment is one of the most joyful, peaceful emotions we will ever experience.

One of my favorite definitions of *contentment* is "tranquil happiness." It implies some of the words I use to describe a feeling of contentment, such as peace, gratitude, and serenity.

The Apostle Paul had learned and earned contentment, regardless of his circumstances:

> But I rejoiced in the Lord greatly, that now at the

last your care of me hath flourished again; wherein ye were also careful, but ye lacked opportunity.

Not that I speak in respect of want: for I have learned, in whatsoever state I am, therewith to be content.

I know both how to be abased, and I know how to abound: every where and in all things I am instructed both to be full and to be hungry, both to abound and to suffer need. (Philippians 4:10–12)

I've talked with people who have lived a long time—eighty years or more—and they sometimes smile as they think back on the chaos of earlier years when there was so much going on in their busy lives. Perhaps they look at those much younger and whisper, "Just you wait. . . ."

During our seasons of too many "shoulds," "musts," and "have to no matter whats," it's hard to feel content. We may yearn for a season of slowing down, of finding time for contemplation and renewal.

Saint Francis De Sales, who lived in 1567, admonished, "Do not lose your inward peace for anything whatsoever, even if your whole world seems upset." Easy for him to say. But is there a way to do that? Can we really keep our inward peace even in an exceedingly full and busy season of life?

Victor E. Frankl, an extraordinary man who wrote an account of the five years he spent imprisoned at Auschwitz and other concentration camps during the Holocaust, shows that we can find peace, and even a measure of contentment, in the midst of horrific things that happen to us and around us. In his landmark book *Man's Search for Meaning*, he tells of his struggle to find meaning and hope in his days: "We who lived in concentration camps can remember the men who walked through the huts comforting others, giving away their last piece of bread. They may have been few in number, but they offer sufficient proof that everything can be taken from a man but one thing: the last of the human freedoms—to choose one's attitude in any given set of circumstances, to choose one's own way" (*Man's Search for Meaning: An Introduction to Logotherapy* [New York: Pocket Books, 1963], 122).

I've enjoyed talking to family and friends about their definitions of contentment. I love so many of the ideas that they have shared and wish I could include them all. But here are just a few:

My friend Tim says contentment is "joy—a quiet, reflective sort of joy."

My brother Frank expressed feelings that virtually everyone also said in one way or another: "There can be no contentment where there is no gratitude." Gratitude definitely seems to be one of the most critical ingredients for contentment.

I laughed when I read what my friend Melanie sent me in an email: "Contentment is knowing that inside my body is a thin spirit!"

One ingredient of contentment is work. I think back on the man in his yard, in a chair, in the shade, reading.

Looking content. And I think to myself, "He's earned it." Perhaps that's another of the secrets of contentment: The man works hard, and then he *enjoys* the results. It's not just for "show," it's for using and enjoying. I appreciate those who make the world more beautiful.

Sometimes contentment comes with time, with age, with experience as well as conscious effort. I love the look of contentment and peace on the faces of those who have lived a long time, and who seem so fulfilled, so satisfied. There is a certain quality of delight and joy that seems reserved for those who have lived a life that qualifies them to *rest*.

My friend Leanne told me about the peace and contentment that have come to her after she experienced some trials where she was struggling for answers, and then the answers came. Oh, yes. Have you felt that too?

I've both experienced and observed peace and contentment. Let me see if I can describe some of the settings and specific moments that popped into my mind when I asked myself about contentment. I'm hoping I can take you with me. Use your imagination liberally.

• It's summer, and we're fishing with Dad at Navajo Lake in Uncle Leo's boat with the carved dragon head on the front.

• It's a pleasant summer evening, and we're sitting in the backyard at Carly's. There are about six or seven of us, and I have my guitar, and we're singing "Home on the

Range," "Red River Valley," "Don't Fence Me In," and lots of other old favorites.

• We're up in the tree house with some of the other little people in our neighborhood, and we have a simple lunch to share. There's a bit of a breeze, and all is right with the world.

• We're in Sukiman's bamboo home in a Chinese cemetery in Central Java, Indonesia, and there is something so quiet about a village that has no electricity or roads (and thus no traffic except for bare feet and an occasional bicycle).

• It's early morning, before the sun has come up, and it's just us, the birdies, and the quiet beauty of this time of day. We're outside, taking deep breaths of fresh air.

• We're near the ocean, and we feel the waves inviting us to get into that steady rhythm, to slow down and calm down.

• We're watching the snow fall and cover everything up. It's one of those quiet storms where the snowflakes are huge, and they seem to fall in slow motion. Everything is getting so beautifully white.

• We're at the top of Mount Timpanogos, and we can pretty much see the curve of the earth. Oh, the view! There's something about being up that high and looking down and around on so much beauty that takes your breath away. (It might also have something to do with the altitude.)

I'm hoping you're thinking of some of *your* specific

experiences where you felt particularly peaceful and content.

You've probably heard or seen the "Serenity Prayer" used in many twelve-step programs. It goes like this: "God grant me the serenity to accept the things I cannot change, the courage to change the things I can, and the wisdom to know the difference."

This reminds me of a very funny poster I saw that looks something like this:

GRANT ME THE SERENITY TO KNOW WHAT I CAN CHANGE. LET ME CHANGE WHAT I CAN. LET ME ACCEPT THAT WHICH I CANNOT CHANGE. LET ME IGNORE THAT WHICH I CANNOT CHANGE OR ACCEPT. LET ME RUN AWAY FROM THAT WHICH I CANNOT CHANGE, ACCEPT, OR IGNORE. LET ME LOCK MYSELF IN THE BATHROOM, HOLD MY HANDS OVER MY EARS, AND HUM ABOUT THAT WHICH I CANNOT CHANGE, ACCEPT, IGNORE, OR RUN AWAY FROM. LET ME BITE THOSE WHO CAN CHANGE, ACCEPT, IGNORE, RUN. LET ME BE!. . . .

Something like that. Hope you had some fun with it, and that it doesn't ruin the "Serenity Prayer" for you from now on.

To some, *contentment* and *serenity* may imply just floating and drifting. Letting go. Doing nothing. That's not even *close* to what I mean when I encourage us to be more content. I want to be sure I am not misunderstood on this point!

As President Hugh B. Brown said: "Complacency is a

very grave danger in the Church as well as in the world. We need to be aroused to the fact that there is much yet to do in this matter of gaining our salvation. . . . We need to study more, to think more, to pray more fervently" (*The Abundant Life* [Salt Lake City: Bookcraft, 1965], 169).

Most of those with whom I talked and wrote about contentment agreed that complacency is not a good definition. As my friend Sandi said, "I believe we can be contented and still be striving and working to improve and progress—to become more Godlike and Christlike." Another friend, Peggy, pointed out that contentment requires our will, and complacency doesn't.

Although contentment isn't complacency, there *is* a place in life for what one essayist called "divine discontent." Elder Neal A. Maxwell used this phrase several times, and I like the sense of being content but at the same time recognizing the need for "trying a little harder to be a little better" (as President Gordon B. Hinckley often encourages us). Elder Maxwell wrote: "It is left to each of us to balance contentment regarding what God has allotted to us in life with some divine discontent resulting from what we are in comparison to what we have the power to become. Discipleship creates this balance on the straight and narrow path" ("Becoming a Disciple," *Ensign*, June 1996, 18).

One of the things that makes us peculiar people is that we're trying a little harder to be a little better when we might already be pretty good.

Anyway, I thought I'd better make sure you knew what I meant by contentment early in the book so that you wouldn't be reading along feeling I was talking about complacency in either spiritual or material matters. I will use "tranquil happiness" as a way to define and describe contentment, along with the phrase the Apostle Paul used: "godliness with contentment" (1 Timothy 6:6).

My friend Cynthia wrote that "contentment is a background, or underlying thing. It's the ocean basin that abides the waves and tides of the surface without perturbation. You can be contented and still be engaged, even busy. You just aren't anguishing over what you might be missing (or even not doing) in your life."

On a trip to Sweden in July 2004, I saw a ship that helped me learn about the need for this balance. In the early seventeenth century, Sweden was at war with Poland, and the Swedish king was in the process of strengthening his navy. He ordered four new warships built, including one called the *Vasa*, which was to be the mightiest warship ever built up to that time. The king himself dictated the measurements, and no one dared argue against him.

It took three steady years and hundreds of craftsmen to build the *Vasa*. The ship was 226 feet in length and had 10 sails, 64 cannons on two gundecks, and could hold 450 men. The *Vasa* began her maiden voyage on Sunday, August 10, 1628. The beaches all around Stockholm were filled with spectators, including foreign diplomats. This was to be a glorious day.

The mighty ship set sail and fired a salute. There was a sudden squall, and her gun ports, which were still open from having fired, went below water level—and the water gushed in. To everyone's horror and disbelief, the glorious and mighty warship suddenly sank! It took only moments for her to disappear below the water, just 100 yards from shore.

The people in charge of the inquiries concluded that the ship was well built but badly proportioned. The cargo—the huge guns—were placed relatively high up in the ship. Deep down in the *Vasa*, several tons of stone were stored as ballast. They were meant to give the ship stability. But they were not enough as counterweight to the guns (weighing approximately 100 tons), the upper hull, masts, and sails.

On the morning of April 24, 1961, 333 years after the *Vasa* sank, and after six years of work, the ship was brought to the surface, and the work of restoration and preservation began. It is housed in a museum built for it. I was impressed to look at something that had been built almost 400 years earlier!

I did a lot of thinking about this ship. For some reason it reminded me of the parable of the olive tree, where the lord of the vineyard and his servant are examining trees that have brought forth wild fruit. The lord of the vineyard is asking: "What could I have done more? Have I slackened my hand, that I have not nourished it, and digged about it and pruned it and stretched forth mine hand almost all day long? What could I have done more for my vineyard?" (see Jacob 5:47).

The servant's response is so instructive: "Is it not the loftiness of thy vineyard—have not the branches thereof overcome the roots which are good? And because the branches have overcome the roots thereof, behold they grew faster than the strength of the roots, taking strength unto themselves" (Jacob 5:48). The root system could not support the heavy, strong branches.

The servant and his master went to work doing some replanting, and they worked to make the root and the top equal in strength (see Jacob 5:66). The analogy for me is that I need to sink my roots deep into the gospel of peace and contentment, making sure my branches don't get so big with pride, with self-importance, with "stuff and things," that I tip over and sink.

Now for one of the crossroads in my life, a time when I learned a little something about pride. It was 1985, and I'd been asked to give what I considered to be a very important talk to a group of women I admired very, very much. When I asked about a topic, they said they wanted me to share the things of my soul. And when I asked about how much time they wanted me to take (anticipating they'd say about ten to fifteen minutes) I was told to take forty-five minutes.

Oh, how I worked on that talk! I typed and typed, and then did a whole bunch of cutting and pasting. I prayed, pondered, searched, typed, cut, pasted, taped . . . and the days went by and the rough draft grew and grew. For some reason I kept that rough draft. Maybe I felt it would be an important reminder for me someday. It looks as if someone has gone through paper from a shredder, trying to put it back together again.

At about this same time, I was informed that the Missionary Training Center (my employer) was going to purchase a couple of computers, and would I like one of them. "Oh, no thanks. I'm getting along just fine with my typewriter." I had one of those fancy electronic ones—surely a computer couldn't be any better or faster than *that*. And I had at least five "pinwheels," or whatever they were called, to give me different fonts. I could type pretty fast, and there was a correction ribbon for when I made mistakes.

After the computers had been purchased, I was approached again. Would I mind keeping one in my office? No, not really. That would be all right. I was still content with my typewriter, but I began to get curious about this computer. Little by little I started using it more and the typewriter less.

I remember specific events, like the day I learned to move a whole block of material from one place to another—a very quick, efficient "cut-and-paste." I also remember learning to switch back and forth between screens.

Now, what if I had not learned to use a computer? I'll tell you this much—I may not have been working on this book right now without a computer. I cannot comprehend or describe the difference it has made for me to know how to use a computer. I'm so *thankful* that I was curious enough to begin experimenting, and that I recognized pretty quickly that I'd found a powerful tool for the kinds of things I needed and wanted to do.

Here's the "pride" part: Before I learned to use a computer, several people said to me something like: "Once you begin using a computer, you'll wonder what you ever did without one. You'll *never* want to go back to a typewriter." Maybe pride came in. I think that is a high possibility. I remember thinking in some part of my heart, "Oh yeah? Well let's just *see* if your computer can keep up with my typewriter!" I had to eat my words, so to speak.

I think of how long it took me to get online—to start using MEE-Mail. (I know most people call it email, but I can't resist using my initials.) I send and receive mail to and from many states and even from places like Africa, Indonesia, the Philippines, Sweden, Germany, Australia, China, Russia, Brazil . . . imagine! And now, sure enough, I don't know what I'd do without MEE-Mail and all the things possible on the thousands and thousands of web sites. I have visited at least fifty of them!

Yes, there will be people who use the internet and other technologies for evil. But we can't let that stop us from jumping in and using the wonderful things that have been invented and developed. Sometimes I can almost feel Heavenly Father looking down and remarking, "The kids are excited again!" As if to say, "You haven't seen anything yet!"

He wants us to have, enjoy, appreciate, and share the good things of the earth. This includes more than just food, clothing, and shelter. It includes technology, for things like working on family history online. (Have you gone to lds.org or familysearch.com recently?)

Brigham Young taught:

> Much can be said upon the doctrine of life and salvation, but I will say this to the Saints in this place concerning the workings of the kingdom of God upon the earth—all good comes from heaven, all good is of the Lord; whatever promotes the happiness of mankind and the glory of God, whatever increases peace and righteousness upon the earth, and leads the people in the way of godliness, comfort, contentment and enjoyment, and tends to increase health and wealth, and life here and hereafter, is of God. (In *Journal of Discourses* 17:115)

Through all these years of pondering the gift of contentment, I've wondered if there could be one most important ingredient. If there is, I think it would be obedience to God's commandments. Living the gospel of Jesus Christ with faith and diligence, doing our best to become more Godlike and Christlike, will bring us the greatest contentment in our lives.

In November 1965, Maria Von Trapp was invited to speak at Brigham Young University. I was teaching nursing at BYU at the time and saw the flyers about Maria's visit. To tell you the truth, I wasn't sure I wanted to go. I had so recently seen the movie *The Sound of Music,* and, to me, Julie Andrews was Maria. I wasn't sure I wanted to change (or spoil) that image.

But curiosity got the best of me, and I went. When she stood up to speak, she captured me with her greeting. Read this with a German accent if you can: "My dear, dear friends." That was it. I was "hooked." I opened my heart and learned so much.

> If you, all of you, would ask me now, right now, after all these years—after those forty years, and a lot of things happened in those forty years—"What do you say now, what is the most important thing in life?" with all that is in me, with all my heart, with all the emphasis to say it, I would tell you, the most important thing in life is really to find out what is the Will of God, and then go and do it.

> When He created us, He created us with a special plan, for a special job and for a certain purpose. And we have the great freedom to say yes or no. If we say no, that job won't be done and that place won't be filled, because we cannot be substituted. We are only one. If we say yes, we will always be happy; we will have that precious peace of mind, peace of soul and that great thing all the magazines and newspapers talk about, and that books and libraries are written about—security. We will never have to worry. Once we know this is what we want, we will also know He

will help us to do it. This is really the hinge around which the life of the Trapp Family is turning. This is what I brought into the house, into the family—that was my dowry. (*BYU Speeches,* November 18, 1965)

I will always remember her advice to find out the will of God and then go and do it. So many with whom I've spoken have said this is a source of great contentment and peace for them: to know that where they are and what they are doing is right. This helps me not to put unreasonable demands and expectations on myself, but to do my best and enjoy my days and experiences.

Elder Marvin J. Ashton said:

> Peace is not a purchase away. Peace is not when the final installment is paid. Peace is not when marriage comes nor when all the children are enrolled in school. Peace is not when the last child returns from the mission field. Peace is not when an inheritance is received. Peace is not when the scars of death start to heal.
>
> True peace must not be dependent upon conditions or happenings. Peace must stem from an inward contentment built upon trust, faith, and goodwill toward God, fellowmen, and self. It must be constantly nurtured by the individual who is soundly anchored to the gospel of Jesus Christ. Only then can a person realize that the trials and tribulations of daily life are less important than God's total goodness.

Lasting peace is an eternal personal quest. Peace does come from obedience to the law. Peace comes to those who develop character and trust. ("Peace—A Triumph of Principles," *Ensign*, November 1985, 70)

I want to go back to the scriptural reference I used earlier in this chapter. The Apostle Paul, you'll remember, has spoken of having learned to be content no matter what his circumstance. He then writes: "I can do all things through Christ which strengtheneth me" (Philippians 4:13).

This last verse reminds us again of one of the primary sources of peace and contentment, doesn't it? What kind of hope would we have, let alone a perfect brightness of hope, if it weren't for the Savior Jesus Christ?

The knowledge of the Savior's life and mission, of the Atonement, and of His love for each of us is the foundation for learning to be content "in whatsoever state I am." Full or hungry, we know Who is watching over us, and that we are part of His fold.

Enough Is Enough

Can you remember hearing the phrase "enough is enough" in your life? Maybe we don't use it as much as we once did, but I can remember hearing it a lot when I was younger. It usually meant, "Stop it! Quit it!" Ha. We'd be quarreling or screaming or throwing silverware or whatever, and Mom would say, "Enough is enough!"

What might that little phrase mean in terms of "stuff and things"? Does it help you understand the title of this book: "You can never get enough of what you don't need"? I like to add to that, "Because what you don't need never satisfies."

To have enough is to be satisfied. It's a point at which you consciously realize you have what you need, and you stop wanting, working, and whining for more. Remember the way it's expressed in the Lord's prayer? "Give us *this day* our *daily* bread." Enough. Sufficient. And if there is an extra loaf, we will share.

To never get enough of what you don't need brings a desire to keep acquiring and accumulating. In such a state, you never feel you have sufficient (probably because what you do have is not bringing satisfaction and contentment). Can you hear Peggy Lee singing, "Is that all there is?"

My friends Bob and Mim shared this story about a man who owned a restaurant that was open six days a week for lunch:

> The food was great and fairly priced and his restaurant became very popular. The owner was able to work during the day and be home with his family on Sundays and all evenings. A wealthy business consultant ate there one day. He asked to speak to the owner and told him that his restaurant could be a gold mine. He suggested that by staying open for dinners, he could triple his profits and become very wealthy. The restaurant owner said, "I don't need more profit. I have enough." The man was astounded by his answer and replied, "You don't understand how wealthy you could be!" The owner replied, "You don't seem to understand that I have enough."

Elder F. Burton Howard explained: "Some equate the good life with economic prosperity and believe that consumption brings contentment. But the effort to achieve prosperity often prevents consideration of the great questions of life, including asking ourselves when enough is enough—and when it is too much. We sometimes discover too late that God's greatest gifts cannot be purchased with money" ("Overcoming the World," *Ensign*, September 1996, 13).

When was the last time you received a bill from the sun? The moon? The stars? The rain? The sunflowers? A sunset? I love a poster I saw that had this message: "Good news! Sunsets are free! (Plus tax) (Plus shipping and handling)"

I hope you can follow what I'm trying to say even when I mess it up with nonsense. God's greatest gifts really cannot be purchased with money, can they? The purchasing power of heaven has nothing to do with earthly coins and paper.

In the book of Acts, we read of a man called Simon, who was a sorcerer, who wanted to buy the priesthood power of the Apostles so that he could lay on hands and bestow the Holy Ghost. "But Peter said unto him, Thy money perish with thee, because thou hast thought that the gift of God may be purchased with money. . . . Thy heart is not right in the sight of God" (Acts 8:20–21).

Is *my* heart right with the Lord? Am I high-centered on the false assumption that consumption brings contentment, and that I can buy my way to happiness and peace of soul?

Why is it sometimes hard for us to reach a point where we realize and acknowledge that we have enough? Why doesn't this happen more easily and more often? Is it greed that keeps me from the satisfying (and satisfied) feeling of having enough? Do my "wants" get out of control? That sounds like greed. Yuck.

Can you think of anything that you have a lot of but that you still keep collecting, purchasing, and acquiring? If I didn't think you'd go overboard and hurt my feelings, I'd give you the names and phone numbers of a few friends who could keep you entertained for quite a while with a list of the things I have more of than I need. It's actually embarrassing.

Here's just one example. I figure if I'm asking you to ponder things that might bring some discomfort, I might as well open myself up and let you know more about MEE. The following was written by someone who knows me well:

> You have way too many updated, outdated, and duplicated church publications; old clothing that has some sort of sentimental value attached (stuff that would fill at least 24 cedar chests); gifts people gave you through your whole life that could go to others or to DI; all kinds of things that are sentimental to you from missions, from the MTC, from trips you've taken, from friends from faraway places; 37 boxes full of every single letter anyone has ever written to you in your entire lifetime—make that 57—maybe 157; probably 89 boxes of pictures (and no, that does not include those little boxes of slides or the slide trays); and books . . . I'm talking file-box size, 41 stacks 3½

feet high each of precious books—precious because
they were either your dad's, your mother's, another
relative's, or yours as a child; you have every single
visual aid and the lesson materials to go with them
for every single lesson or class you have ever taught
in your entire life and for over 40 years of teaching
missionaries or being a missionary; that adds up to at
least 3½ tons of visual aids and lesson materials.

Your problem ain't never been buying anything
more than too many pencils, paper, felt-tipped pens,
paper clips, organizers, file folders, pens, envelopes,
9" x 11" x 1½" boxes (which are stacked to the ceil-
ing). You need to stay out of office supply stores—
they are dangerous for you!

Well, since I've opened Pandora's box (praying there is
more hope than evil in it), I might as well go further. Hang
on!

It's about the boxes. I have boxes of every size known
to man (or woman). I have a box for every purpose under
heaven. With other people it might be shoes, or purses, or
gadgets and gizmos. It might be books or magazine sub-
scriptions (and the magazines keep coming and coming).
It could be catalogues or cats, fish or videos or fabric or
thimbles or tools. For me, it's boxes.

I can tell you about specific boxes—where and when I
got them and why I'm so sentimental about them. Boxes
that syringes came in when I was a student nurse. Boxes
Dad brought home that were used for X-ray paper at the

BYU health center. A box in which I sent some souvenirs home from Japan when Charlotte and I were traveling there after my first mission.

I do think my admission about having way too many boxes will make you stare at me in a funny way the next time you see me. Maybe you'll wonder if there's a chance the boxes will gang up for a "boxer rebellion." Maybe you'll ask, "How are your boxes?" and I'll lose all the color in my already colorless face. Maybe we'll laugh. I hope we both do, not just you.

If you're like me, you can rationalize *why* you have so many or so much of something (shoes, fabric, tools, coats, or whatever). "I save these boxes because I've lived in places where I didn't have any." Ha. That's an *excellent* reason to keep so many things around. Sometimes I say to myself, "Self, having this many things is not helping one single other person on the planet! Get a life!"

Dissatisfaction—not feeling you have enough—is a very troubling feeling. It's the feeling that you need "just one more." "Just one more pair of shoes and *then* I'll have enough." (You can't use that line; Imelda already did.) Just one more CD, one more book, one more tool, piece of luggage, one more car . . . any minute now I'm going to have enough.

Let me tell you of an experience I had many years ago. I was thinking about luxury. What is luxury? I asked myself. I decided I'd make a list. As I look back, I think I was feeling that one of something was a necessity, but two or more would be a luxury. One was enough! So I started listing things that it would be a luxury to have two of.

I started by writing down "two homes." That was a good place to start. I know one place this might have come from. I probably heard someone praying at the close of a meeting on Sunday, "Take us to our various homes in safety." Various homes? How many do you have? I imagined the family in the foyer of the chapel trying to decide which home was best for that day. "Oh, Daddy, Daddy, I want to go to 'Home B,' it has the biggest TV screen!" Isn't that ridiculous?

But I think that's where my list started, writing down "two homes" as I considered my own definition of luxury. Two homes. Oh yes, it was working. One home was a necessity; the second would be a luxury. One was surely enough.

Two cars. Same thing. Luxury. I was getting it now! Two TVs. I was on my way to a deeper understanding of luxury! Pure intelligence was flowing into my brain and my heart. I couldn't wait to tell everyone else what I had discovered and learned! Two this, two that. The list got longer and longer. I was on a roll!

And then it happened. A whispering—no, it was louder than a whisper—from inside. The still small voice, but louder than usual (sometimes that's the only way I can really hear), was saying, "When did you stop saying *luxury?*"

"What?"

"When did you stop saying that two of something was a luxury?"

"Oh . . . I did stop, didn't I?" I knew from that familiar feeling I was getting that I was about to learn something that wasn't necessarily going to be happifying. Do you get those feelings sometimes?

When did I stop saying two of something was a luxury? That was the question that had come into my mind. I wasn't sure I wanted to think about what the answer revealed about me.

I stopped saying "luxury" when *I* started having two of something! Had you already figured that out? It was probably the "two phones" place on the list. I could *easily* explain to someone why I needed more than one phone. More than two. More than three, even. As President Ezra Taft Benson used to quote, "There, there, little luxury, don't you cry—you'll be a necessity by and by."

Oh, so it's only a luxury when someone *else* has more than one, is that it? Wow . . . is that the way I think? Is that the way I live?

Here's what I learned. Two of *anything* is a luxury. Two friends, two meals in one day, two "free" hours of time . . . it's *all* luxury. We are blessed beyond measure. We are blessed beyond our ability to realize or count.

I began to think it might be helpful to take an inventory of what I had. Would this be helpful for you too? Don't make this too big a deal, too exhaustive or exhausting. But would it be helpful to know what we have? What if we counted the number of shoes we have? Or the number of coats or tools or gadgets or unfinished projects.

So, how many pair of shoes do I have? I know we likely would say "pairs of shoes" these days, but I grew up when we used just "pair" as plural, and it's hard to shake some of these habits. How many would be enough? Could we decide on a number?

I suppose I could never go back to my childhood and have just three pair: one for Sunday, one for school, and one for play. No. Because now there are shoes for *everything*. And they're not just for "utility," they're for decoration as well. And for torture. I'm sure of that as I watch the dangerous circumstances of women perched four or five inches off the ground on nail-sized heels. Yikes!

Somewhere I have kept a full-page ad from a newspaper showing perhaps thirty different pair of shoes, each with a different function. There are shoes for golf, basketball, tennis, bowling, kick-ball, dancing, night-crawler hunting, and, it seems, for a whole bunch of other things like jogging, running, climbing trees and phone poles, walking, walking fast, skipping, walking slow, sitting, playing hopscotch (I don't really remember exactly what was on the list) . . . it was a "wow!" kind of experience.

So no, I couldn't go back to having just three pair. For one thing, I'm not going to school anymore. So I asked myself again (realizing I had tried to run away from the question): "How many pair of shoes is enough?" I still don't have an answer. I'm not kidding. I thought, "Well,

could you get along with double your childhood limit—
could you get along with six pair?"

Okay, I say to myself, I'll never have as many pair of
shoes as Imelda, but I have *way too many*. It's interesting to
me how many times I'll compare *up* instead of *down*. In
other words, I'll say that I don't have as many pair of shoes
as Imelda. Well, *duh*. One time she was confronted with
the rumor that she had 3,000 pair of shoes. She said no,
that she only had 1,060. Many of those shoes are now in a
museum in Manila! And not long after she and Ferdinand
left the Philippines, she cheerfully reported that she'd purchased another three hundred pair.

Anyway, I need to do more comparing *down* instead of
up. There will always be someone somewhere who has
more than I do. But there are far more who have less than
I do. "Even in Japan," writes my friend Tim, "one of the
most advanced countries in the world, people get by with
so much less than we do here. They get by with less space,
less free time, and a lot fewer material things like boats and
fancy cars, and they don't seem to be any 'less happy' for
it." My dear friends Zoe Leone and Clayton Petty, who
served as missionaries in Tanzania, East Africa, wondered
if children with expensive, fancy toys were any happier
than children they saw with toys made out of whatever
discarded materials they could find.

It makes a difference to compare down instead of up,
but that's not really the point I'm trying to make. What I

want is to come to a point where I realize I have enough—regardless of how it compares with what someone else has.

Here's a pondering question I ask myself: "What *really* satisfies you? Of all the 'stuff and things' you have in your home, which of your possessions make you the happiest?" And then I think about it—a lot. What comes to your mind when you ask yourself that question? A new car? A raise? Winning? When it's time to harvest the garden? Making something? You know, when I talk to myself about it, I conclude that it doesn't take a whole lot to satisfy me. But is that evident in the way I live? Is it really true?

I think, "What an incredible time to be alive!" Not only do we have electricity and indoor plumbing, we have a way to heat our homes in the winter and cool them in the summer! We have remote controls for almost everything, including the garage door and our entertainment center. We have washers for both clothes and dishes. Some have microwave ovens, hot tubs, and flat-screen TVs with more than 100 channels and TiVo. There are computers, printers, copiers, scanners, and FAX machines. For keeping in touch with each other and the world as well as keeping track of information, we have cell phones, pagers, PDAs, broadband internet, T-mobile, BlackBerry, and on and on. Woweee!

But, as President James E. Faust has said: "The relationship of money to happiness is at best questionable. Even the *Wall Street Journal* acknowledged, 'Money is an article which may be used as a universal passport to everywhere except heaven, and as a universal provider of everything except happiness'" (*To Reach Even Unto You* [Salt Lake City: Deseret Book, 1980], 8).

Brent Top, a professor at BYU, has written:

> Whatever worldly thing it is that we may covet—zealously striving to obtain and then retain—never seems to bring an end to our desires. Covetousness, envy, jealousy, and greed always escalate into a vicious spiral, as we seek greater and greater gratification but find less and less contentment. . . . Striving to acquire the things of the world not only does not bring lasting happiness and peace, but it drives us to seek more. When "all we've ever wanted" is grounded in the temporal trappings of this world, it is never enough! ("Thou Shalt Not Covet," *Ensign*, December 1994, 25)

So how can we know when we have enough? I have some friends who decided, during a time when they had very little money, to make a list of what it would take to make them feel "rich" so that they would recognize it when it happened. It included things like having a reliable car to drive and having their home paid for. They find that it's helpful to look at that list now and realize how rich they are.

I loved a conversation I had once with my young niece Noelle. She and her husband were just starting school; they had three little ones, and finances were very tight. Noelle said they pondered a lot about how to make ends meet. One day she came up with this thought: "What do we do with our money *now* that we'll do *always?*" She wrote on a card (which she still has): "I have as much money as I am ever going to have. I AM RICH."

She reminded me of feelings I've had about generosity. If a person is going to be generous, there are "signs and symptoms" all along the way. It's not about the amount of money one has so much as it's about the condition of the heart. Some of the most generous people I have ever met have had *so little* in the way of "stuff and things."

Many call this an abundance mentality. It's the opposite of the scarcity or inadequacy mentality. In that state of mind, we'll never reach a point where we can be generous. Some who have tremendous resources horde what they have, and it ends up cankering them (yuck!).

"Wo unto you rich men, that will not give your substance to the poor, for your riches will canker your souls; and this shall be your lamentation in the day of visitation, and of judgment, and of indignation: The harvest is past, the summer is ended, and my soul is not saved!" (D&C 56:16).

In the twelfth chapter of Luke, the Savior shares with His disciples a parable about a foolish rich man who had a great harvest and ran out of room in his barns. Instead of sharing—realizing that all he had belonged to God, not him—he hoarded. He apparently didn't think he had enough. He built bigger barns! And then he decided to "eat, drink, and be merry. But God said unto him, Thou fool, this night thy soul shall be required of thee: then whose shall those things be, which thou hast provided? So is he that layeth up treasure for himself, and is not rich toward God" (Luke 12:16–21).

He hoarded and coveted his fruits and goods, and he lost his soul! And perhaps he was still whining, "All I want is a little more than I'll ever have."

Contrast that with the mood expressed in these verses from the Doctrine and Covenants:

> I, the Lord, stretched out the heavens, and built the earth, my very handiwork; and all things therein are mine.
>
> And it is my purpose to provide for my saints, for all things are mine.
>
> But it must needs be done in mine own way; and behold this is the way that I, the Lord, have decreed to provide for my saints, that the poor shall be exalted, in that the rich are made low.
>
> For the earth is full, and there is enough and to spare. (D&C 104:14–17)

The Creator teaches us that the earth is full, with enough and to spare. And I sometimes change the last word slightly and say we have enough and to share. Or enough *if* we share.

We do have enough and to share. It helps me to hear this question in my heart as I'm trying to simplify and share: "Is there someone who could use some of these things, some of this stuff? Is there someone who might need them more than I do?"

My niece Wendy Sue writes:

> I think the best way to share is to give away just enough that it stings a bit, then keep giving over time until it becomes easier and you can give more. Keep bumping up against the threshold. You'd be surprised how much you can give, even on a tight budget. It's like any other habit. Generosity is a habit that can be developed. If you don't have money, give time. Another great way to give is to look at what you truly use. If you have not used it for a long enough time, you should give it away. It keeps the clutter down and spreads items to those who truly use them. I am a big believer in DI, Goodwill, and Salvation Army donations.
>
> Some giving will be harder than other kinds of giving. I think talents are often the easiest thing for me to give. Teaching someone a new skill is a form of giving that comes easily, while monetary donations right now are fairly difficult because of our student-style budgeting. I still do as much as I can. I suspect that later in life the time/money ratio will change, and time will become harder to give.

I love it that she includes the sharing of time and talents. If you have only one talent, that is more than enough if you will get busy applying and sharing it. It could be that as we become increasingly generous, we'll realize that we're closer to having everything than we realized. We may even reach the contented feeling of lacking nothing.

It may be useful, either alone or with family or friends, to consider ways in which Heavenly Father has blessed you both spiritually and temporally. It also might be interesting to share with each other your answer to which of the material things you have in your home (apartment, condo, tent) make you happiest and most content.

Maybe you're lucky enough to have grandparents or other relatives or neighbors who have lived longer than you have, and perhaps it would be interesting to invite them to your home to talk about what was "enough and to spare" when they were little people.

Perhaps you can find stories from ancestors about some of their enjoyment as well as their challenges. And it might even be fun to discuss what the title of this book means: "You can never get enough of what you don't need." Add to that the thought: "Because what you don't need never satisfies."

Okay. That's enough!

Materialism

My brother Frank gave me a "Far Side" cartoon that I think expresses perfectly the theme of this chapter. You know how cows are often used as a symbol for contentment. This cartoon shows a cow couple in their luxurious home. Mr. Cow is sitting watching TV with a can of some liquid beverage (probably not milk) in his right hoof and a ring in his nose. Mrs. Cow is standing by the window, all decked out in false eyelashes and jewelry. She's saying, "Wendell . . . I'm not content."

The point is made so clearly there: Materialism and contentment are not compatible. The very word—*materialism*—is kind of an unsettling one for me. Any time you put "ism" on a word it sounds like a disease. Or maybe like a hobby or topic about which we've become exceedingly zealous, even almost "consumed."

And materialism *is* about consuming and consumption (which is, I think, the word that was used for tuberculosis in the olden days). I'll tell you this much: I've become exceedingly aware of and concerned about it.

What do you think it means to be materialistic? What *is* materialism? Have you heard phrases like "binge buying," "luxury fever," and "conspicuous consumption?" What do they mean? Are they connected to worldliness?

I said that adding "ism" is like saying something is a disease. If that's true, am I sick of all my "material"? No, I'm not talking about fabric this time . . . I haven't taken up sewing yet. Settle down. I'm talking about all my "stuff and things."

I really do love the word *stuff*. And I really do have a *lot* of stuff. Does it make me sick? Perhaps. Does it push me toward greed and selfishness? It really might.

Materialism, to me, means placing a higher value on material possessions and income than you do on your personal relationships (including with your family and with your Heavenly Father) or your spiritual and physical well-being.

Elder Dallin H. Oaks wrote:

> When attitudes or priorities are fixed on the acquisition, use, or possession of property, we call that condition materialism. . . .
>
> From the emphasis given to this subject in the scriptures, it appears that materialism has been one of the greatest challenges to the children of God in all

ages of time. Greed, the ugly face of materialism in action, has been one of Satan's most effective weapons in corrupting men and turning their hearts from God.

In the first of the Ten Commandments . . . God commands: "Thou shalt have no other gods before me" (Exodus 20:3). This . . . commandment is a comprehensive prohibition against the pursuit of any goal or priority ahead of God. The first commandment prohibits materialism. (*Pure in Heart* [Salt Lake City; Bookcraft, 1988], 73–74)

It seems as if materialism is connected with dangerous companions such as greed, secularism, overindulgence, vanity, pride, a lack of charity, and selfishness. Whew. That's quite a list. It also breeds anger and other unhealthy emotions.

Actually, I'm afraid of getting this particular disease. I'm afraid of materialism. I think it's highly contagious. I've had the feeling for a long time that if I don't become more aware of it and root it out of me, it's going to smother me. It's going to create in me some ways of thinking and some habits that will be hard to change.

Materialism can become a kind of bondage, a trap. It involves acquiring stuff and things, and living perpetually in what I've come to call the way-too-fast lane.

President Ezra Taft Benson pleaded with us to study the Book of Mormon, to notice the lessons there are for right here and right now, and to live by the principles taught therein. He wrote: "And more than anywhere else, we see in the Book of Mormon the dangers of materialism and setting our hearts on the things of the world. Can anyone doubt that this book was meant for us and that in it we find great power, great comfort, and great protection?" ("The Keystone of Our Religion," *Ensign,* January 1992, 7).

President Brigham Young worried about this very thing a century and more earlier. "The worst fear that I have about this people," he said, "is that they will get rich in this country, forget God and His people, wax fat and kick themselves out of the Church and go to hell. This people will stand mobbing, robbing, poverty and all manner of persecution and be true. But my greatest fear for them is that they cannot stand wealth" (James S. Brown, *Life of a Pioneer* [Salt Lake City: Geo. Q. Cannon and Sons Co., 1900], 122–23).

Can *we* stand wealth? Can *I?* I've thought about President Young's statement concerning the ways in which becoming rich can change us. I wonder, for example, if my feelings are blunted, or if there's the chance they could be even while I'm not paying attention.

Sometimes when I'm pondering all of this it annoys the dickens out of me. I want to scream! "Hey, I don't have *nearly* as much stuff and things as _____!" And I name someone on the list of the 100 richest people in the world. Well, duh . . .

My best pondering is when I look carefully inside, not just outside. How's my heart? Am I drifting away from the awareness that *all* I have is from God, and doesn't really belong to me anyway?

This drift toward materialism is illustrated clearly by the cycles in the Book of Mormon, as my friend Sandi reminded me. She said she'd been teaching from the book of Helaman, where the cycles are so dramatic and frequent. "Things are going so well. There is business and trade and the Nephites and Lamanites are living together and everything is going great. Folks prosper and there is peace in the land. Then bingo—some folks start getting greedy—wanting more, wanting more, wanting more . . . and presto, back come the secret combinations, the sins, the wickedness, the wars, the murders, and so on."

This cycle has been described as righteousness and prosperity, which leads to pride and wickedness, which leads to destruction and suffering, which leads to humility and repentance, which again leads to righteousness and prosperity. Fascinating!

Where are we in the cycle? This could turn into a very interesting discussion, perhaps with friends or family members or anyone else. I find it thought-provoking even to think and talk to myself about it—Where am I personally?

President David O. McKay shared the following observations. As you read, keep in mind the year he said this (1934):

> I have noted recently something which has given me great concern. I have thought that I have detected

in men and women who have called upon me and whom I have met in my travels just a little evidence of discouragement, and yet it is our right to be happy. It is the destiny of man to have joy.

But the quest is unfulfilled in the search for material treasure. If the experience of the past few years has taught us anything, it has taught us that it is unwise to seek happiness in worldly possessions only. I say "only" because I do not minimize the value of the material things of the world as contributing factors to man's peace, joy, and contentment. The Lord himself has said that if we worship him with rejoicing and prayer, with glad hearts and cheerful countenances, the fulness of the earth is ours. (See D&C 59.) (In Conference Report, October 1934, 91–93)

My friend Cindy shared the following with me, comparing her life when she was growing up to her life as it is currently:

I grew up in what would be described as lower-middle-class or poor circumstances. We had seven in our family and lived in a small, 800-square-foot home with all five of us children in one bedroom. We had two sets of bunk beds and a twin at the foot of those beds. Everyone in the neighborhood was of the same means, maybe a little bit better off.

It was not until I reached high school did I realize

we were poor when I had to wear my K-mart outfits and hand-me-downs. It was okay, though.

What I do remember were parents who had time for me. My father was an avid outdoorsman. And he took us everywhere with him. We were his friends. We went fishing, hiking, camping, boating, picnics in the park, snowmobiling, etc. I forgot to mention those special times when we were able to stop for an ice cream cone on the way home.

I now live in a 2.5 million dollar house. I sat on the sofa after this last move, exhausted and drained. There was so much to do, and again, another night slipped by that I was not able to read to my children because other things took priority.

I am constantly a slave to the lifestyle. I have 10,000 square feet to clean, mounds of washing, laundry, yard work of four acres. When does it stop? Perhaps it is because of my blue-collar background, but I have difficulty paying someone to do all this work.

Sadly, the time with my children is lessened not only because of the demands on me but because they are off on the third floor or somewhere. I can't find them!

I thank Cindy for sharing so honestly, and I hope we can learn something from and with her.

Some of you may have seen the same story I saw zipping around on the internet. It tells of an American businessman in a small coastal Mexican village. He was at a pier when a small boat with just one fisherman docked. Inside the small boat were several large yellowfin tuna. The American complimented the Mexican on the quality of his fish and asked how long it took to catch them. The Mexican replied only a little while.

The American then asked why didn't he stay out longer and catch more fish? The Mexican said he had enough to support his family's immediate needs. The American then asked what he did with the rest of his time. The fisherman said, "I sleep late, fish a little, play with my children, take a siesta with my wife, Maria, stroll into the village each evening where I play my guitar and sing and talk with my amigos. I have a full and busy life, señor."

The American felt he had a better idea, and suggested that he could really help the fisherman. "You should spend more time fishing and with the proceeds buy a bigger boat. Eventually you could buy several boats, until you would have a fleet of fishing boats. Instead of selling your catch to a middleman, you would sell directly to the processor, eventually opening your own cannery. You would control the product, processing, and distribution. You'd need to leave this small coastal fishing village and move to Mexico City, then LA and eventually NYC, where you'd run your expanding enterprise!"

The Mexican fisherman asked, "But señor, how long will all this take?"

The American replied, "Fifteen to twenty years."

"But what then, señor?"

The American laughed and said, "That's the best part. When the time is right you would announce an IPO and sell your company stock to the public and become very rich. You would make millions. Millions!"

"Then what, señor?"

The American said, "Then you would retire. Move to a small coastal fishing village where you could sleep late, fish a little, play with your children, take a siesta with your wife, stroll into the village each evening where you could play your guitar and sing and talk with your amigos. . . ."

Sometimes the disease of materialism makes us so discontent that we spend our lives searching for that which is already very close and very precious.

As a nurse, I have had many opportunities to observe people who were dying make the journey from here to There, and I have learned so much. It is a holy thing, and for those who are aware of what is happening, it is a time for thinking of that which matters most. That's when I've noticed that people speak of their greatest treasures, including their relationships and sweetest memories. I don't remember anyone ever saying that they wish they'd had a better computer or a nicer wardrobe.

Several friends have said they tried the experiment of imagining that they had just a few months to live. One friend said this was an exercise presented in a lesson in Relief Society. Those who wished to should ask themselves what they would spend time and other resources on if they had, say, just six months to live. It's a fascinating experiment.

I've done this more than once, feeling a couple of times that it might be "for real," and I didn't think much about material possessions. I mainly thought about relationships—people I wanted to visit, friends I wanted to express love and thanks to. I don't need to go into detail about this, but if it's something you haven't tried, I think you'd find it very interesting.

It's similar to imagining that you're to be abandoned on a desert island. Now this always makes me laugh when I hear that phrase, since islands are mostly tropical, not desert. But either way, you're going to be alone. And you can take a small suitcase full of anything you'd like to have for the year you'll be gone. The question is: What do you put in your suitcase?

Some who've experienced disasters teach me a lot about what matters most to them when they describe having made sure all their family members were safe and then grabbing, not trinkets and clothing and jewelry, but family pictures, journals, genealogy charts, family history, and such.

My friend Stephanie shared a wonderful idea about working with her husband to teach their children the values they wanted them to develop, including the avoidance of materialism:

> We have a nightly family ritual. After scriptures
> are read, prayers are said, and children are tucked

into bed, the last thing we say to each child is, "I love you more than . . . (some object of importance or value)"

The child then repeats with his or her own, "I love you more than . . ."

I have learned that I am loved more than ice cream, my son's favorite toy car, my daughter's favorite doll, dad's pickup, flowers, sunshine, and even the stars. It has become quite the game as each child tries to think of a new response each night.

Our children need to know that they are loved more than the house, the car, or our favorite hobby. They need to know that we value them over any worldly possession.

It may be a meaningful discussion to ask ourselves what is most precious (priceless, even) to us—what do we most cherish? And how do others know that? I visited a home once where the living room was off-limits to the children because of the light-colored carpet and elegant furnishings. Perhaps it shouldn't have been called the "living" room. It seemed more like a "not-for-living" room. Maybe they were just keeping it separate from the "family room," where the children *were* allowed.

Jerry Mason, in a very helpful article in the *Ensign*, asked, "Do we avoid using money to compensate for not spending enough time with our children? Substituting gifts for parental involvement encourages materialism and may confuse children about the difference between love and money" ("Setting a Good Financial Example," *Ensign*, September 1999, 71).

Does our fascination with accumulating, possessing, and consuming affect our relationships? Many say yes. I know that there are times when relationships seem to be perceived in the language of money: "Is he or she worth the trouble?" Or, "I have too much invested in this relationship to just walk away."

Elder Jeffrey R. Holland spoke of the dangers in some of our trends.

> In almost every direction, we see those who are dissatisfied with present luxuries because of a gnawing fear that others somewhere have more of them. . . . In an absolutely terrifying way, we see legions who say they are bored with their spouses, their children, and any sense of marital or parental responsibility toward them. Still others, roaring full speed down the dead-end road of hedonism, shout that they will indeed live by bread alone, and the more of it the better. We have it on good word, indeed we have it from the Word Himself, that bread alone— even a lot of it—is not enough. ("'He Hath Filled the Hungry with Good Things,'" *Ensign*, November 1997, 64–65)

In all my reading and thinking, in all my observing and experiencing, I have come to feel that the essence of life is not what it so often *seems* to be—working to have, working to get, working to possess. It's about *becoming*. It's about what's happening *inside* of us. *Being* is so much more significant and happifying than only *seeming*.

I know it's nice to make my environment, including my home, conducive to peace, beauty, enjoyment, and contentment. I also feel that it's important not to let anything become more important than my relationship to my Heavenly Father, the Savior, my family, and other fellow travelers on this interesting, challenging road back Home.

I believe that all of God's commandments, including the one where He asks us not to put anything else in place of Him or in front of Him, but to keep Him in "first place," are designed to bring us blessings, including a wonderful life, genuine happiness, peace of soul, and a perfect brightness of hope.

You may already have a list of things you want to think about or do. Is it wrong to be wealthy? When does it become wrong? Are there some activities and discussions that might help us as individuals and families to avoid materialism? Can we detect any attitudes or habits that could lead us away from what matters most to us? I have no desire to make anyone mad or even uncomfortable. I just want us to be more aware, more thoughtful. There are things I want to do differently in my life, and perhaps they are some of the same things you might be working on. Maybe we can work together!

Our Treasures and Our Hearts

et's start this chapter with some questions. What say
ye? (That was a question.) Here's another: What are
your most priceless treasures? I was going to ask,
"What are your most treasured possessions?" but somehow the other question seemed better. I want the question
to get you thinking (and perhaps even making a list).

Another way to ask the question could be: Where is
your heart? I think this means a lot of things, including
what we seem to cherish the most, to give our time and
attention to—what we try to hold on to and protect.

I am putting treasures and hearts together because of
what the Savior taught in Matthew 6:19–21:

> Lay not up for yourselves treasures upon earth,
> where moth and rust doth corrupt, and where thieves
> break through and steal:

But lay up for yourselves treasures in heaven, where neither moth nor rust doth corrupt, and where thieves do not break through nor steal:

For where your treasure is, there will your heart be also.

Let's see if we can find out where some of those safe places are—places where there aren't any moths, and there's no rust (maybe even no dust!), and thieves can't get in.

Sometimes it might be easier to find where our hearts are and, by doing that, we would discover our treasures. At other times, we might start by finding out what and where our treasures are, and then we would discover our hearts. Maybe there would be some surprises and discoveries either way.

This is, in many ways, like an actual treasure hunt. We're hunting for our treasures as well as our hearts. And, as in most "hunts," there are clues.

When I was a little girl on First West, I used to love to make maps to imagined treasures. I would send my friend Zonie or my sister Charlotte or anyone else who would go along with the game on a treasure hunt. I remember wishing I could put the clues on soft, rolled-up leather, written in black paint, like I'd seen in the Saturday matinee.

My clues were written on paper, and then I'd crumple them up to try to make them look old and mysterious, even exotic. I never did have anything very valuable to hide or find, but I loved the idea of searching for treasure.

I'd dream about big caves where pirates had stored gold, silver, jewelry, crowns, and lots of bright and beautiful things like I'd seen at the "five and dime."

I also loved finding coins, especially in the couch and chairs when Grandpa visited, and in the field after the carnival had been to town. For the short time in my life when I believed there really *was* a pot of gold at the end of a rainbow, I would daydream about finding it.

But let me go back to clues before I get carried away with the rainbow thing.

Suppose I'm searching for my treasures. What are the clues? Let's see. Maybe one clue would be: Where do I put things? What is in a prominent place? Is there anything behind glass and "locked in"? Anything with a light shining on it? Anything that almost never comes out of a safety deposit box? Anything for which I pay more in insurance than I do in fast offering?

Another clue might be: "Where do I spend the most time?" It might be at the office, with the children, at the bowling alley, or doing various chores. (Oh, don't you hope we can take our chores to heaven with us?)

For some it might be outside, daydreaming in the hammock, digging in the garden, making the yard more beautiful (or at least more visible—part of my yard is hidden by weeds). For some it might be with books, the internet, a piano, a car, video and computer games, scrapbooks, or a horse.

Is your heart in your "portfolio"? Your bank account?

Your golf bag? Is it wrapped in an old, cherished quilt? Is it in your stack of all the things your children have brought home from school and church?

Is your heart with your collection of swans and walnuts? Is it in all the goodies in your fridge and freezer? Is it in the shiny car that you keep covered in your garage and seldom use? Your coin or stamp collection? Your new computer with more gigs than you can shake a mouse at? Your riding lawn mower that plays music and massages your back?

Is your heart in your child's smile? Is your heart with your grandchildren? Can you hear the little ones arriving, shouting "Papa! Papa!" Look for your heart and consider your treasures. Enjoy!

Let's say I'm going on a personal treasure hunt in my home. Hmm. If I'm going to think first of only "stuff and things," I'll tell you that I really treasure the painting of the Savior done for me by my brother-in-law Wendell in about 1986. It's hanging in my home. It's so beautiful. He not only painted it, he designed the frame. To me it's priceless. It's one of the first things I checked on when I had a Big Bad Flood in 2000. And it wasn't damaged in any way (miracle).

And by the way, that flood is one thing that set off a whole ton of thinking on all of the subjects in this book! (And yes, since you asked, many of my carefully hoarded cardboard boxes did get very, very wet, and some were ruined to the point that they had to be thrown away. I sobbed myself to sleep on more than one occasion and dreamed of cardboard.)

Other treasures include my missionary journals. I went looking to see how they were as I sloshed through an exceedingly wet home on that terrible night. My journal of my mission in Indonesia got wet, but not ruined. The other journals remained safe and dry.

There were other things I checked on, and some treasures had to be thrown away. That wasn't easy.

But the more I think about it, the more I realize that my greatest treasures are not so much "stuff and things" but precious, priceless intangibles. Memories. Loving relationships. Experiences. Deep feelings about the Savior and the Atonement. Things I can take with me when this part of my journey is finished.

It's been fun reading about and asking others what they want to take with them when they go Home—or, as some like to say, when they "shoot on over."

Elder ElRay L. Christiansen told of a wealthy man in Denmark who was converted to the gospel and had migrated to Utah. His commitment caused the loss of much of his fortune, but, after settling here, he again had the ability to amass riches and, in the process, lost his faith and testimony.

As his brethren tried to counsel him about his eternal purpose, he would not listen. Finally one of them said to him, "Lars, it is not good to think only of money. You cannot take it with you, you know."

Lars answered, "Vat is that you say?" and he was told again, "I say you cannot take it with you."

Lars responded, "Vell, den, I vill not go."

Elder Christiansen's report was that he had gone anyway. (Wm. Grant Bangerter, "The Quality of Eternal Life," *Ensign,* November 1988, 81)

My sister Charlotte told me a little story that caused me to think. It seems there was a wealthy man who was distraught about the thoughts of dying and leaving all his treasures behind. He'd worked so hard and accumulated so much!

So he somehow made a bargain with a Heavenly Official. He could pack one suitcase full of anything he wanted to take with him. It would not be taken away from him when he "checked in." (See, I'm treating it kind of like a hotel experience.) After considering carefully what he wanted to take, he filled the suitcase with gold bars.

When he got Over There, St. Peter was waiting, and was curious about the case. "Mind if I look inside?" he asked. The man wasn't pleased about this and insisted that he had special permission to bring it with him. St. Peter assured him that he only wanted to see what he'd chosen to bring—that he wouldn't take it away. He opened it up, looked inside, then seemed amused. "Why in the world would you bring pavement?"

One reason I like this joke is because it reminds me about how *different* it might be when we leave this world, leaving behind so much that has come to seem so important, even critical, while we're here.

Money can't buy happiness or peace or anything else worth having—anything that will go with us when we leave. But we continue to love phrases like "show me the money!" By contrast, the Apostle Paul counseled us to "Set your affection on things above, not on things on the earth" (Colossians 3:2). The prophet Alma counseled one of his sons: "Seek not after riches nor the vain things of this world; for behold, you cannot carry them with you" (Alma 39:14). And Nephi's little brother Jacob taught:

> But wo unto the rich, who are rich as to the things of the world. For because they are rich they despise the poor, and they persecute the meek, and their hearts are upon their treasures; wherefore, their treasure is their god. And behold, their treasure shall perish with them also. . . .
>
> Yea, wo unto those that worship idols, for the devil of all devils delighteth in them. (2 Nephi 9:30, 37)

President Spencer W. Kimball helped me understand that passage better in his remarkable and unforgettable message "The False Gods We Worship." I encourage you to read and ponder the entire article. I look at idol worship and the first two of the Ten Commandments in a different way since reading and studying his message. He said:

> [Some] have submitted themselves . . . to the enticings of Satan and his servants and joined with

those of "the world" in lives of ever-deepening idolatry.

I use the word idolatry intentionally. . . . I am more and more convinced that there is significance in the fact that the commandment "Thou shalt have no other gods before me" is the first of the Ten Commandments. . . .

The Lord has blessed us as a people with a prosperity unequaled in times past. . . . Do we have more of these good things than our faith can stand? Many people spend most of their time working . . . to *guarantee* carnal security. . . . Forgotten is the fact that our assignment is to use these many resources . . . to build up the kingdom of God . . . to bless others in every way, that they may also be fruitful. Instead, we expend these blessings on our own desires, and as Moroni said, "Ye adorn yourselves with that which hath no life, and yet suffer the hungry, and the needy, and the naked, and the sick and the afflicted to pass by you, and notice them not." (Morm. 8:39.) . . .

To set aside [all of God's great promises] in favor of a chest of gold and a sense of carnal security is a mistake in perspective of colossal proportions. To think that [we have] settled for so little is a saddening and pitiful prospect indeed; the souls of men are far more precious than this. (*Ensign,* June 1976, 4–5)

Can you read a phrase like "a mistake in perspective of colossal proportions" from a prophet and not have a need to understand why he would say that?

I remember going with a friend to her grandmother's home a few days after her grandmother's funeral. So many treasures were still there. We talked about what she'd left behind, but also what she had taken with her. I remember thinking that somehow Heavenly Father would have let her have a garden in heaven—she'd worked so hard and made her yard and garden so beautiful.

But all her "stuff and things" were still there, right where she'd left them. I wondered what her memories had been during her life as she looked at her beautiful things.

One day my mother and I sat going through drawers in one of the rooms of her home, deciding what she wanted to do with each thing. We came across such treasures as her lifetime pass to attend any athletic event held at Fullerton High School. She earned this because of her love of sports and her abilities, especially with tennis. It was so much fun having her reminisce about these childhood memories.

We found many other things as well—nothing huge or expensive in terms of monetary value, but such sweet treasures. You know what I mean, the things that are worth nothing and yet are worth everything. It was a genuine trip down Memory Lane. I'm so glad I was able to accompany her that morning.

You know, it might be interesting for us to pretend that *we* had been given permission to take a suitcase when we leave this world (don't bargain for a trunk! I already thought of that), and we could put anything inside we wanted. I actually have a feeling that most of us would choose genuinely precious things and not "pavement."

I like what my friend Glen said about what he wants to take with him:

> Well, hopefully, we'll remember some good experiences—experiences that enriched our lives. Our relationships go with us, along with our identity, our sense of right and wrong, and our senses of humor and whimsy, our ability to play and work and enjoy both, our reverence for Deity and respect for fellow man. I hope to retain our physical skills—even in such areas as sports. I hope to enjoy differences in personality and appearance and even accents. Wouldn't it be sad to lose all of the differences? Like our differing accents? And senses of humor?

He helped me realize that I hope the same thing—that we'll retain some of the qualities and characteristics that make us unique and that we so enjoy in others.

My friend Debi wants to take the trust, respect, and love of her loved ones, and all the completed ordinances for every family member they can find (including Debi's dad's great-uncle John Fahy Davis, whom Debi's looking for . . . so if you have *any* information on Uncle John, please get in touch with MEE and I'll let Debi know). My sister Charlotte and Art, her husband, want to take their family, their love for the Savior, knowledge to replace faith, and priesthood blessings from the ordinances and covenants (and the desire to help others have those as well).

My brother-in-law Art said, "When I close my eyes for the last time I will see the best friend I've ever had: my beloved wife." For many people, their greatest treasures are already on the Other Side, waiting for them. I love talking to my mother about that. "When you see Dad again, he won't be ninety-five with a cane, hearing aids, and no hair—he'll be the handsome young doctor you fell in love with back when you were both so much younger. And then you'll have a great big surprise when you realize how *you* look—that you are the beautiful young nurse he fell in love with."

Isn't it an incredible feeling to know that what we've been taught is *true* and *real?* I love knowing that there *is* a life after this one.

I think of the parable of the Ten Virgins. Our oil is what we need, and it consists of all our kindness and faithfulness, our love of the Savior and service to and for Him, our deep conviction of His life and mission, of the reality of the Atonement, of the beauty of Heavenly Father's great plan of happiness, of redemption, of salvation.

And as we do work for others that they cannot do for themselves in holy temples, can you imagine how it will be to eventually meet them! I used to tell the missionaries it would be a great door approach: "Hello, I did some very important work for you while I was on the earth—would you like to know more?" I picture many amazing reunions as we meet people for whom we have done sacred work in temples.

Some have mentioned that they don't have a whole lot of earthly treasures—that the most important work they've done is to learn how to get back Home to their Heavenly Parents and other dear loved ones, and to send their treasures ahead as much as possible "where moth and rust can't corrupt."

Elder Rex D. Pinegar told of something that happened to a faithful family in Texas. Brother Donald Pinnell was at church when someone told him his house was on fire. He and his family had recently built their dream home on their Texas ranch. Now he and his two sons were racing to that home, not knowing what they would find:

> As he and his boys approached the top of the terrain, they could see in the distance the smoke coming from their burning home. Donald Pinnell said of that moment, "We could tell that our home was completely engulfed in flames; and I just stopped the car at the top of the hill for a few minutes. I said to my sons, 'Now look, you can spend all your life storing up treasures of the earth, and you can sit on a hill and watch them go up in flames, or, you can store up the right kind of treasures and take them with you through eternity.'"

The right kind of treasures are our families and those divine attributes and qualities of character that are taught and learned in gospel-centered homes.

May we make the necessary individual and family course corrections which will put the Lord and our families first and fill our homes with these eternal treasures. ("'Home First,'" *Ensign*, May 1990, 11)

In the New Testament there is an account of Jesus being approached by a rich young man who asked what good thing he could do to have eternal life. The Savior reviewed some of the basic commandments, and the young man replied that he had done all of those things since he was a little boy. So the young man asked another question and received a response he couldn't seem to handle.

> What lack I yet?
> Jesus said unto him, If thou wilt be perfect, go and sell that thou hast, and give to the poor, and thou shalt have treasure in heaven: and come and follow me.
> But when the young man heard that saying, he went away sorrowful: for he had great possessions. (Matthew 19:20–22)

Elder Joseph B. Wirthlin said that "the man went away sorrowing, for he loved his possessions. . . . How many of us would pass this test?" ("The Straight and Narrow Way," *Ensign*, November 1990, 65)

He's asked us a question. How do we answer it? Would I pass this test? If I would be perfect, if I would be made whole and complete, what would I give up? To what lengths would I go to follow the Savior? What is it I'd have trouble letting go of?

Proverbs 15:16 states: "Better is little with the fear of the Lord than great treasure and trouble therewith." I don't know that it matters whether we have a lot or a little, but I *do* think it matters where our hearts are in the whole scheme. What is *my* heart set upon? What and where are *my* greatest treasures? Are there moths in them, and rust, and dust? Or are they safe?

Think of times when you've read something in the scriptures like, "Behold, my joy is full." Perhaps in Third Nephi, chapter 17, one place where the Savior expressed that (see verses 20–23). Why was His joy full? Had He just received an incredible gift from the surviving people in the Americas? No, His joy was full because His lap was full— of little children. He took them *one by one* to bless them and love them. He asked those observing to behold the little ones. Behold them *one by one*. Individually. Each a precious treasure.

Remember how full of joy Ammon was (in Alma 26)? Was it because the Lamanites, now converted to the truth, had given him and his companions a bunch of fatlings of every kind? No. He had a chance to be a king, as did at least one other brother, Aaron, and neither of them accepted that honor and responsibility from either the Lamanites *or* the Nephites. Their joy was full because they had helped thousands of their brothers come to a knowledge of their Savior and Redeemer.

These converted Lamanites were willing to bury their weapons of war, and I'm thinking they didn't make "treasure maps" on leather or crumpled brass plates or anything else so that they could go back and find these weapons when they changed their minds. Their minds, their hearts, had changed away from that way of living. They really meant it!

Where does *my* joy come? What are the moments in my life when *my* joy is full? Do I ever unconsciously say something like, "Behold, my joy is full, because I have a lot of stuff and things?" I don't think I do, but do I without realizing it? Do you ever catch yourself thinking or saying something like that? It might not start out "Behold, my joy is full." It might start out "At last!" or "Oh, George, come and look!" or "I can't wait to have the people who drive by notice . . ."

My friend Rachael talked about a time recently when two of her college-age children came home for a visit, and they watched a movie together and then sat and talked and laughed a lot until after midnight. She said:

> There was such a feeling of peace, and joy, and calm assurance that all was right in my world, at least for a short period of time. Over the years I have watched my children grow and learn and make good, righteous decisions, and those are times of contentment, too, knowing that they have assimilated at least some of the gospel doctrines we have tried to instill in them. As John says, "I have no greater joy than to

hear that my children walk in truth" (3 John 1:4). Then I feel content; I feel like I couldn't ask for anything more, as the Gershwin song goes!

Knowing that our Heavenly Father has a specific plan whereby our obedience brings joy and so many other treasures, listen again to the message in Matthew 6:33: "But seek ye first the kingdom of God, and his righteousness; and all these things shall be added unto you."

Here's the way the verse appears in the Joseph Smith Translation, Matthew 6:38: "Wherefore, seek not the things of this world but seek ye first to build up the kingdom of God, and to establish his righteousness; and all these things shall be added unto you."

As we search for our hearts and our treasures, the Source of all good blessings has given us a wonderful clue or map: Seek *first* the building up of His kingdom, and to establish His righteousness, and *then* all these other things shall be added.

In all my studying, pondering, and writing, I've come to the conclusion that much of my gravitation toward certain earthly treasures is because I just do not yet understand what it means when the Savior says, "all that my Father hath." I'm so tied to, so accustomed to, and so smitten with some of the great "stuff and things" I have as an Earthling that it's difficult for me to imagine the "riches of eternity" right now. I don't know how to imagine or even dream about what that might mean.

Elder Sterling W. Sill used some verses from the

Doctrine and Covenants to teach something about these riches.

> "For he that receiveth my servants receiveth me;
>
> "And he that receiveth me receiveth my Father;
>
> "And he that receiveth my Father receiveth my Father's kingdom; therefore all that my Father hath shall be given unto him." (D&C 84:36–38.) If you can think of something more exciting than that, I don't know what it would be.
>
> God is a very wealthy personage. We all like to inherit from a wealthy parent, and what could be more exciting than to inherit from God, to get everything that God has. Someone has said that thrift is a great virtue, especially in an ancestor. And God has been very thrifty, he has also been very wise and he has been very generous. ("A Fortune to Share," *Ensign*, January 1974, 61–62)

The Lord gave some important counsel to Emma Smith through her husband the Prophet Joseph Smith, recorded in Doctrine and Covenants 25:10: "Lay aside the things of this world, and seek for the things of a better."

Isn't that a sentence worth pondering? Seek for the "things" of a better world. Look forward and press forward, keeping a steadfastness in Christ and with a perfect brightness of hope (see 2 Nephi 31:20).

Here's a little exercise I'd like to suggest: Try going from room to room in your house on a kind of treasure hunt, looking and thinking and talking (to yourself if there's no one else around, but this could also be a great discussion with others) about which of all the things you have is most treasured, and why. Remember that lots of treasures are on the *inside* rather than on the *outside*. Think also of specific treasures you have stored in heaven. Think what it is you *can* take with you.

I think what we take with us is trust—trust in God, in the Savior, in all that we've been taught and all we've learned. We trust that in the next life we *will* have rest and peace, and all that we need for that kind of living. Ha: "that kind of living." Oh, haven't you read things about what it's going to be like, and for memorable moments you've been able to let go of all that is worldly?

When it's time for me to "shoot on over," I guess it all boils down to this: I want to take my heart with me, in the figurative sense. I want to take a pure heart. I want my treasure to *be* my heart—all that it's felt, all the reaching out to others, all the tenderness and kindness, all the searching and discovering, and all the joy.

Choices

We live in a culture that seems to bombard us with messages about things that will make us better, happier, more popular people if we're able to own them. As a result, many people are never satisfied.

What are we really buying? We buy necessities such as food, clothing, and shelter—things having utility. But when we start to spend more than necessary in any of those categories, we may be trying to buy something else, such as happiness or status. Maybe we want to keep up with the latest fad or trend. That happens often when we make an impulse purchase.

Try this: Take a little time to be conscious of the incredible choices available to us. It might be fun to ask your children or friends to list as many different kinds of breakfast cereal as they can think of in one minute, for example. Smaller tots might need two minutes and some help. Give the "winner" a Pop Tart.

See how many fast-food places or motel chains you can name in a minute. How many different TV stations can you come up with? Or how many different airlines, flavors of ice cream, sports, automobiles, elevator companies, or varieties of tomatoes? You get the idea.

We *do* have a lot of choices, don't we? Whenever I have come home from an experience in another country, particularly in one of those places we call "developing," I've gone to stores just to look around. I've wandered up and down the aisles (probably looking lost, or like I just came in off the island with Robinson what's-his-name).

It blows me away to see what a *variety* we have. Let's say you go to the deli part of a store (if they have one—don't try this at Checker Auto Parts) and order a sandwich. Then they say, "What kind of bread?"

"Uh—a couple of slices will be fine."

"But what *kind?*"

"Well . . . uh . . . what kinds do you have? Anything in brown, black or beige?"

They go over the list of kinds of bread, and it makes you want to laugh. Wheat, White, Sourdough, Rye, Thick, Thin, Fresh, Day-old, Cheesy, Pumpernickel, Sesame Street (I think it's really Sesame Seed) . . .

By the time they finish talking to me about meat, cheese, pickles, olives, lettuce, mayo, mustard, onions, sprouts, seeds, watercress, spinach, beans, shipping and handling, and other doo-dads, I've almost forgotten where I am and why (but I'll still eat).

So yes, we do have a *lot* of choices. Is this *good* for us? I think it's a blessing, but can it also be a burden? How do we keep from taking too much of our time just trying to decide?

Do some choices matter more than others? Even as I ask that, it seems like the answer is a pretty loud "YES." How do we decide which decisions matter most? Ha ha. Are you getting caught in a loop here?

Here's a little exercise I did for my own interest. In thinking about choices, I looked around at magazines, newspapers, books, catalogues—all the things from which I can choose what I want to read. I wondered what guides my choices. Where do I spend the most time in my reading—what kinds of articles attract my attention?

I decided to do some checking, some comparing. I wanted to broaden my search beyond what I had at hand, so I borrowed a variety of magazines from others, and I looked in some at stores. Talk about choices!

I'm going to list some things I can read about in different magazines. You might guess what some of the magazines are, but I'm not going to tell you. This isn't about specific magazines so much as it's about how I spend my time—what I choose to read. And if you think this list is a bit long, you should have seen it before I chopped it!

Here, in no particular order, are some of the titles of magazine articles I found: "The Plot Against Elvis," "The

Tall and Short of Politics," "Fall Cruise Spectacular," "Why Do Men Cheat on Beautiful Women?" "Hotel Ratings Made Simple," "Draft Watch: Quarterbacks," "Standing in Holy Places," "Easing the Pain of Osteoarthritis," "Bald Eagles Come Back from the Brink," "Smashing New Looks for Fall," "Britney's Mega-Makeout Session," "A Voice for Values," "Putting Ethics Before Science," "The Shoe Fetish," "The Lifeline of Prayer," "Countdown to a Bikini Body," "A Husband's Secret," "The Corvette You've Always Wanted," "Building a Better Wireless World," "More Money, More Freedom, More Fun," "The Law of Tithing," "What's New, Who's Hot, What's Next," "Taming Haywire Computer Cords," "Stars' Funniest Prom Stories," "The Dawning of a Brighter Day," "How the Boomer Vote Will Rock America," "Stepping into the World of Norman Rockwell," "Focus on Fathers."

Here I am with seemingly endless choices of things I can bring into my home, my life, my mind and heart, my memory. I can choose to be enriched or entertained, to be informed or distracted, to be enlightened or darkened. These are the things from which I pull ideas to ponder. It's all stored somewhere inside of me.

I can consciously work to read and study things that will add to my contentment rather than promoting a feeling of dissatisfaction or envy. I can create and nurture feelings of gratitude, joy, compassion, awe, reverence, charity, and so on. I can learn so much that will be interesting and useful to me. It's up to me!

Is there a chance—a caution, maybe—that our lives are being filled with so many choices that we're sinking in the middle? Have I realized lately how much time I spend in my *TV Guide* trying to decide if there's anything I want someone to tape for me? (See, I just have the six or seven basic channels, so I miss a lot of good stuff on History or Discovery or A&E. And I really do want to have BYU-TV in my home one of these days when I'm around more to watch it.)

Larry A. Tucker, in an article about the influence of television in our lives, wrote of the depiction of an opulent lifestyle:

> Affluence and power are common themes of some of the most popular shows on current prime-time television. Some programs consistently glamorize materialism and glorify "the things of this world." (See D&C 121:35.) With high-fashion wardrobes, luxurious estates, and insatiable appetites for wealth, these TV characters portray the false idea that greed brings gratification and that "the natural man" (see Mosiah 3:19) is happy. Life-styles portrayed on these programs often promote self-satisfaction rather than sacrifice, greed instead of charity, and conceit rather than humility. ("What's on TV Tonight?" *Ensign*, February 1988, 19)

In his article "Why the Devil Takes Visa," Rodney Clapp writes: "A key component of today's [consumerism] is the proliferation of choice. Grocery stores that two decades ago stocked 9,000 items now stock 30,000. Many homes have 50 or more TV stations to choose from (and not much worth watching). How many of our choices are actually significant?" (*Christianity Today*, October 7, 1996, 19–33). I read that and have been wondering if the number of items *now* in stock has gone from 30,000 to, say, 50,000 since 1996. Wowee! And I think the number of choices for TV stations is well beyond 50 or even 100.

So I begin wondering if I have so many consuming choices to make each day—what to eat, wear, watch, read, surf (as in "on the internet")—that there's the danger I'll be left without enough time or energy for prayer, scripture study, temple attendance, pondering, time with family and neighbors, and so on. Does the process of making so many choices steal too much of my time?

And here's another worry I have. Living to consume (and collect, acquire, possess) rather than consuming to live seems to foster some values that seem opposite to the values I'm trying to develop. If I want something, and I want it *now,* can I still develop the ability to deny myself? Can I still develop patience? And self-control?

I have heard the story of parents who brought a newborn baby before Robert E. Lee, asking his advice as to what they should teach the child. "How should he make his way in the world?" And the wise old general said, "Teach him to deny himself. Teach him to say no" (see Jeffrey R. Holland and Patricia T. Holland, *On Earth As It Is in Heaven* [Salt Lake City: Deseret Book, 1989], 130).

As I've studied and pondered contentment through the years, I've come to recognize that advertising *does* have an influence on me. I've recognized that sometimes I get a feeling of not being satisfied with what I have.

I don't know if it has the same effect on all of us, but there are so many times when I see something advertised—maybe on TV, in a magazine or newspaper, on a billboard, in a store—and I'll think to myself, "Self, I must have that! Look how wonderful that is!" It's almost as if life cannot go on unless I have this particular thing to add to my supply of stuff.

And I am amused by seeing things in stores with big labels on them: "As seen on TV," as if that assures quality and will help us find what we were looking for. If you'd bought it when it *was* seen on TV, though, they would have thrown in the extra set of steak knives at "no extra charge." This is great, having so many products say "15% more free." "Today only." "No payments until the next eclipse!"

Once I saw a cartoon showing a guy driving a nice convertible, probably headed home from shopping. He has a huge box in the backseat. It has the name of some computer thing he's purchased, and it's model #5.0 or some such number. He's whistling, smiling, and looking very happy, content, and satisfied.

But then he sees the billboard. And on the billboard is an advertisement for the very product he just purchased. There's a man on a scaffold doing the unthinkable: He is pasting a big 6.0 on the top of the 5.0. . . . And the driver of the convertible just lost his happiness, his contentment, and his satisfaction.

Hey, there will always always always be something newer, better, more powerful, more amazing. How do we find contentment in a world like ours where so many products are marked "New!" "Improved!" "More bubble action than ever before!" It's true with cars, watches, TVs, computers, clothing, even breakfast cereal. "Has 19% more fiber than the leading brand!" "More teeny tiny marsh-mallows than you can ever count!" "Fewer grams than a piece of paper!" (or a piece of cardboard).

It's not like I want to start an ad agency and begin advertising, "Enjoy what you have," but that is something I'd like to recommend highly to myself (and to you, if it would make a difference for you like it does for me).

Some of the ads I've saved seem to promote the opposite of "one heart, one mind" and "hearts knit together in unity and in love." One shows a woman with a beautiful diamond bracelet and necklace. The ad reads: "Now you can't say you haven't a thing to wear. Nothing else feels like real gold. Nothing else makes any moment so precious."

Another ad reads, "Separate yourself from the rest of humanity." Wow. And then there's the one for a special chewing gum: "At last! Chewing gum for the rich!" I saw some once and tried it, and I say, "Let the rich have it!" To me it tasted kind of like a cross between cough medicine and Mr. Clean.

I ran across a letter to the editor a few years ago that caught my attention. It began, "What's the world coming to when ads teach young people not to share?"

A man speaks of having watched two commercials that made him sick:

> One . . . was a candy bar commercial which depicts a twin, riding a bike, running her sister into a tree so she doesn't have to give her one of the two bars that come in the package. It ends with "Two for me, none for you."
>
> The other was a snack-chip commercial in which the main theme is "Get your own bag." What is happening here? How can we expect our youth to ever experience the value of sharing, let alone the joy it instills in both the giver and the receiver. (Chip Lee, Cedar Rapids, Iowa, in *USA Today*, February 26, 1998)

What messages are children receiving as they watch hundreds and thousands of advertisements on TV, and are surrounded by other kinds of advertising? Here's just one distressing example:

> MasterCard is using a shopping-themed Barbie doll to boost its image among children as young as 3. The "Cool Shoppin' Barbie" . . . comes with . . . all the equipment children need to pretend Barbie is shopping in a store—including a Barbie-sized credit card with the MasterCard logo. A . . . spokesman said

"It empowers children to play out a realistic shopping adventure."

But some say the doll makes children think credit cards are toys. When the card is pressed into the . . . card scanner, Barbie's voice singsongs: "Credit approved!" They fear that sends the wrong message when consumer debt is soaring. A record 1.3 million personal bankruptcies were filed last year. [More people filed for bankruptcy than graduated from college.]

One woman [author Gerri Detweiler] said . . ."If they really want to educate kids, they would include a bill and make them fork over interest payments." (Kara K. Choquette, in *USA Today*, March 30, 1998)

I know there might be one of these dolls in your home, and I'm not knocking Barbie, but I am very interested in the concerns expressed.

In an article from *Newsweek* about the need for parents to learn to say no to their children, I found the following:

Today's kids want much more, partly because there's so much more to want. . . .

[Children] are responding to a tidal wave of marketing aimed at kids. According to the American Academy of Pediatrics, the average American child sees more than 40,000 commercials a year. That's in addition to fast-food outlets in schools, product placements in TV shows and movies, even corporate sponsorship of sports stadiums.

"There's virtually no escape from it," says Susan Linn, a Harvard psychologist and the author of "Consuming Kids: The Hostile Takeover of Childhood."

"The marketers call it 'cradle-to-grave brand loyalty.' They want to get kids from the moment they're born." ("The Power of No," *Newsweek,* September 13, 2004)

Do you get a lot of catalogs in the mail, especially starting a few months before Christmas? Do you ever wonder how some of the companies get your name and address, and why they keep sending the catalog to you when you have never ordered a single thing from them?

When you get a catalog in the mail with a message like, "This could be your last one!" (unless you order something), don't you sometimes wish they were serious? One of my favorites has the following message: "Final catalog: We won't bother you with unwanted catalogs . . . we'd rather save paper and trees. So this could be your last issue. Please order today if you wish to receive future issues. If you Want Not, we'll Waste Not."

They always seem to leave an opening: "This *could* be your last issue." It might not be, if you hurry and order something, or if we think you might order something in the future. And I do still get mailings from some companies from whom I've never ordered a single thing. How do they know I haven't moved to another country, or that I'm not dead?

So what's the point? The point is that we all have been given the gift of agency, of choice. It is in the exercise of this agency—the ways in which we choose—that we develop our character, becoming more (or less) like the Savior, and choosing (perhaps not always consciously) between contentment and a lack of it, between having enough and wanting more.

President James E. Faust talked about choices in general conference:

> In this life we have to make many choices. Some are very important choices. Some are not. Many of our choices are between good and evil. The choices we make, however, determine to a large extent our happiness or our unhappiness, because we have to live with the consequences of our choices. Making perfect choices all of the time is not possible. It just doesn't happen. But it is possible to make good choices we can live with and grow from. ("Choices," *Ensign*, May 2004, 51)

To conclude, here are some individual and group activities you might want to consider:

• How about going to a busy mall (if you have one close enough) and sitting in a place where you can just watch. Observe. And think. Maybe you'll want to walk around and look at all the stores. How are the windows decorated or designed to encourage you to come on in and see if there's something you want? Do some of the posters and other displays seem inappropriate to you? Could you make your feelings known? Which stores pull you most—which have the strongest magnets?

• Maybe you could make up a little game such as, "If you were sent to an island where you'd be alone for several months, what are ten things you'd want to take with you?" Then you might share your lists with each other and ask questions such as, "But could you get along without _____?"

• See if you can rent a copy of the PBS program *Affluenza* and watch it. If you have the chance to watch it with others, have a discussion about what you learned and what good ideas might have come to mind. I have included some details about the program in the Appendix.

• I think there could be some lively family and other group discussions on the proliferation of choices and the influence of advertising on our choices. Would it be interesting for you to have everyone in the family collect some ads or write down a description of what he or she has seen or heard? "Ad Night at FHE." Have a lively, wonderful, interesting, enlightening discussion. Don't forget the "ads" from the *New Era,* by the way; they're certainly powerful in the right direction.

Just becoming more *aware* of the influences around us will, I feel, help us to be more careful and wise in our choices. Choose truth and light. Choose contentment. Choose joy.

Freedom from Bondage

Are you in any kind of "bondage"? Yes, you might say—I'm in bondage to chores, like laundry. Good answer. The daily grind probably *does* sometimes seem like bondage, doesn't it? Dishes, laundry, dusting, reading, yard work, answering letters and the phone, and driving children to and fro are things that *never* seem to be "caught up."

Some of us might think of strong habits, or even addictions, that cause us to feel like we're in bondage. Some of these are so hard to break, to change. These could be anything from gambling to pornography, from alcohol to "soaps," from eating too much to shopping, from tobacco to games, from internet use to unenriching reading. The list goes on and on.

Some may feel in bondage because of the accumulation

of too much financial debt. Whether you are in debt or not, can you think of why so many, including prophets, have called debt a kind of bondage? Have you experienced, or can you imagine what it would be like, living without any debt?

This chapter is going to focus mostly on the bondage of financial debt. What I'm sharing is not meant to give all the answers as to how to be debt-free in a short amount of time, but I do hope to give enough references here and in the Appendix that you'll be able to find some resources if you need them.

When I was about fourteen or fifteen years old, my parents called all of us children together for a short family council. My dad announced that we were completely free of debt. I remember where he was sitting and how happy he and Mom looked.

I know I didn't understand much about why they were so happy, and what it meant to be free from debt, but I felt good inside because I could tell it was extremely important to them.

Now, I also have the blessing of being free from debt, and as I come to the point where I'm going to be on Medicare and receiving Social Security checks (can you believe it?), I think I understand much more about how important that announcement was to my parents so many years ago.

. My brother Frank has some notes from one of the family home evening lessons Dad gave us about being careful with our money. When Frank showed me the notes, I recognized the paper immediately. Dad used to bring home from the health center the gold paper in which X-ray film was wrapped, and that was what we would use for scratch paper. Memories! Dad and Mom were both very frugal. Frank also remembers Dad calling his investments "my little slaves," and teaching us the difference between interest we receive and interest we pay.

Debt *is* a form of bondage. Likely you have jumped ahead of me and are already remembering President Gordon B. Hinckley's powerful message from general conference in October 1998, in which he counseled those attending the priesthood session to "pay off debt as quickly as you can, and free yourselves from bondage." He said: "What a wonderful feeling it is to be free of debt" ("To the Boys and to the Men," *Ensign,* November 1998, 54).

President Hinckley had mentioned debt in an *Ensign* article years earlier:

> It is the labor and the thrift of people that make a nation strong. It is work and thrift that make the family independent. Debt can be a terrible thing. It is so easy to incur and so difficult to repay. Borrowed money is had only at a price, and that price can be burdensome. Bankruptcy generally is the bitter fruit of debt. It is a tragic fulfillment of a simple process of borrowing more than one can repay.
>
> Now, I hasten to add that borrowing under some circumstances is necessary. Perhaps some college students need to borrow to complete their education.

If you do, see that you pay it back. And do so promptly, even at the sacrifice of some comforts that you might otherwise enjoy. Most persons have to borrow to secure a home. Prudent borrowing may, of course, be necessary and proper in the management of business. But be wise, and do not go beyond your ability to pay. ("Thou Shalt Not Covet," *Ensign*, March 1990, 4–5)

President N. Eldon Tanner also gave a significant talk on this topic. The title is one you may recognize: "Constancy amid Change." Here is an excerpt from this powerful message:

> I have discovered that there is no way that you can ever earn *more* than you can spend. I am convinced that it is not the amount of money an individual earns that brings peace of mind as much as it is having *control* of his money. Money can be an obedient servant, but a harsh taskmaster. Those who structure their standard of living to allow a little surplus, control their circumstances. Those who spend a little more than they earn are controlled by their circumstances. They are in bondage. (*Ensign*, June 1982, 4)

President Heber J. Grant taught of the connection between contentment and freedom from the bondage of debt: "If there is any one thing that will bring peace and contentment into the human heart, and into the family, it is to live within our means, and if there is any one thing that is grinding and discouraging and disheartening, it is to have debts and obligations that one cannot meet" (*Relief Society Magazine,* May 1932, 202).

And then there is the interest on debt, and I've read nothing that has been quoted more often on the topic of interest than that shared by President J. Reuben Clark Jr.:

> It is a rule . . . in all the world that interest is to be paid on borrowed money. May I say something about interest? Interest never sleeps nor sickens nor dies; it never goes to the hospital; it works on Sundays and holidays; it never takes a vacation; it never visits nor travels . . . it has no love, no sympathy; it is as hard and soulless as a granite cliff. Once [you're] in debt, interest is your companion every minute of the day and night; you cannot shun it or slip away from it; you cannot dismiss it; it yields neither to entreaties, demands, nor orders; and whenever you get in its way or cross its course or fail to meet its demands, it crushes you. (In Conference Report, April 1938, 103)

Imagine—he taught that back in 1938! It seems to have been a problem all the way along. President Spencer W. Kimball said, "All my life from childhood I have heard the Brethren saying, 'Get out of debt and stay out of debt'" (in Conference Report, April 1975, 166).

There is a phenomenon (I don't know what else to call it) that seems to be increasingly prevalent, even though borrowing and lending have been around "forever." It's called anything from "deferred deposit" to "pre-payday loans" to "cash advance loans" to "payday check service" to . . . well, to loan sharking. You read right. The more I've studied this, the more disturbing it becomes, and the more it sounds like loan sharking to me.

One day I was listening to a news program about it, and the reporter said that the interest on some pre-payday loans runs as much as 927%. You read right again— 927%—in annual interest charges! This is a staggering bit of information! And I've heard it can go as high as 6,205%! You think these are typos, don't you? They're not!

What these businesses do is cash paychecks in advance and give the borrower two weeks to pay the loan back plus a huge fee. And then, if the borrower doesn't pay in time, the person can let the loan deadline "roll over," but then another two-week fee is tacked on. Talk about bondage!

I receive so many things in the mail inviting me to choose bondage. I got a colorful postcard, for example, sent to "Current Resident" (they do know me so well). "The cash you need, interest free.*" (There always seems to be an asterisk beside statements like that.) "Immediate approval! No credit check!" And they say, "Congratulations! You've been pre-approved for an Interest Free* loan. Get cash in minutes!" You bring the card (so they can make sure you're "Current Resident"), a recent bank statement, your personal check and I.D., and off you go into bondage.

What if you really do need help? Are there other places you might go rather than resort to those high-cost alternatives? Could you turn to your family—and be sure to have everything in writing so that both sides know what's expected? (I am *not* talking about a handout, about "something for nothing," but a temporary loan to help you). Could you try for a small loan from a bank or credit union? Could you ask your creditors for additional time to pay the bill (so that you don't need to get one of these shark loans)? Even trying for a pay advance from your employer would seem a better option than getting a short-term, way-high-interest loan.

Here's a fact we all need to realize (this one's not a factoid, it's a big, basic fact): Spending more than we make is always, always a terrible trap. And the short-term, way-over-the-top, high-interest loan is *not* a way to solve this money management problem. Instead, we need to avoid unnecessary purchases—even of small, daily items.

Those who do best with managing their money have learned to budget. Carolyn C. Williams shared some excellent suggestions in an *Ensign* article. She said that some feel as if a budget isn't necessary. For example, there may be newlyweds who don't feel that they spend that much money. But she writes: "Young couples can benefit from establishing good budgeting habits early in the marriage. Even though expenses may be few, simple measures taken at the beginning of their life together lay a foundation that can be built on in the future as financial obligations increase." ("Beginning Budgeting," *Ensign*, April 1997, 71).

There are many excellent programs, including some computer programs, that can help us to become much more aware of where our money is going. This can make a difference in our decisions about where we *want* the money to go. One useful CD-ROM is provided with the little book *Debt-Free on Any Income: A Practical Guide to Financial Security for Latter-day Saints,* by Lyle and Tracy Shamo.

There are *many* groups devoted to helping people get out of debt and stay out of debt. Just in wandering around on the internet, I found many different organization web sites that looked helpful.

I'm going to tell you something that cracked me up. While I was working on this chapter, the phone rang. The Caller ID said "CCC Centers." "Hello," I said.

"Did you know that there is help for consolidating debt?" it responded, and then went on and on. I started to laugh! How did they know? It was a recording, or I could have had a terrific conversation with this company. I had to hang up, though, because I was busy, and I wasn't in debt.

Speaking of budgeting, it's critical to help our children become financially responsible. Someone reading this chapter probably has a son or daughter who's away from home for the first time—perhaps attending a university— and the young person signed up for a credit card from among the many offers he or she was swamped with and is now deeply in debt, wondering what happened.

President N. Eldon Tanner said: "Perhaps parents should be more like the father of the college boy who wired home, 'No mon, no fun, your son.' His father wired back, 'How sad, too bad, your dad'" ("Constancy amid Change," *Ensign*, June 1982, 6).

I met a wonderful couple from Grace, Idaho, who shared the following experience with me. They told me they begin teaching their children financial responsibility when they're very young, and that a significant milestone is reached when each child turns fourteen. At that age, the children are added to the family's bank account, and they can write checks.

They told me of one of their sons who had been signing up for a class or activity at school that required a fee. Those helping him sign up asked how he was going to pay for it. He said, "With a check." They asked if he had one that his parents had signed, and he said no, that he'd be the one writing and signing the check.

One of his friends standing nearby said something like, "Well hey, write it out for more than the stuff costs, and we can get some pizza!" The young man said, "No, you don't understand. The reason my name is on the checks is because I don't do things like that." Wow. What an incredible thing!

They also told me that one of their daughters, as soon as she turned fourteen, asked if she could go with her friend to the local A&W to get something to eat and then write out her first check. Of course.

Later she returned, and was a little quiet about it. But they wanted to know how it went. Rather embarrassed, she said it was going all right until she asked, "How do you spell 'A&W'?"

Family home evening and family council can be effective times to help your children learn the value of financial responsibility. The good habits they develop will serve them well throughout their lives.

President James E. Faust shared a great statement: "When asked how some people in a small farming community in southern Utah got by on their meager cash income, George Lyman said, 'They lived on the absence of expense'" ("The Blessings We Receive As We Meet the Challenges of Economic Stress," *Ensign,* November 1982, 90).

I love that idea so much. "They lived on the absence of expense." Can we cut down on what we spend? Can we live within our means? Can we let go of the competition that sometimes causes us to spend money we don't have to buy things we don't need to impress people we don't even know or like?

Through the years there has been an imaginary family, and it seems everyone has been trying to "keep up" with them. Of course you know who they are: the Joneses. I've been thinking a lot about them as I've been studying and writing. I've come to some conclusions, but they're not facts.

I've concluded that the Joneses have slipped into the background. They became converted to provident living, sold their palace, and moved to a modest home that they have now paid for. Their fancy cars are gone and they have two less expensive cars, both of which are also paid for. They considered changing their name, but they decided to keep Jones and just fade by ceasing to have more than they needed.

So now who gets to be the one we try to keep up with? Actually, it's not a family, as it used to be with the Joneses. It's a whole group of people. We call them celebrities. We cannot get enough of watching them, reading about them, finding out where they got their suit, their purse, their shoes. We are hypnotic about our obsession with wanting to know all about their lives, their bling-bling (what in the dickens is that?), their hairstyle, their current partner, their secrets. No wonder we're never satisfied—how could we ever catch up?

My brother Frank said he feels that "those who are content can generally live on any income, but the discontent are never satisfied on any income (no matter how much they make)."

The control you exercise over your money has just as much to do with your financial happiness and contentment as how much money you have. The more control you have, the less money you need to live and be content.

My brother Richard gave me a newspaper article years ago that reported on the results of a survey. People who worked along or near Wall Street in New York City who made around $500,000 a year were asked questions to find out if they were happy, if they were satisfied.

Perhaps you can guess the answer: They were not.

They were neither happy nor satisfied. With $500,000 a year? Right. And the reason? You may already have guessed it: They knew people who were making *more* than $500,000 a year—people who had more "stuff and things."

I was thinking of a question: "What would it be like if we didn't have to worry about money?" At first I was probably thinking of myself and wondering what it would be like to be *rich* (maybe like Scrooge McDuck) and not have to worry about money.

Then it hit me that perhaps there are many who have *tons* of money who ask the same question. They may look at those living a much simpler, less complicated life and ask, "What would it be like if we didn't have to worry about money?"

As you consider your own circumstances, how about sharing your personal feelings about the importance of financial responsibility. Do you have experiences that would illustrate the principles you want to teach? Ask others (family members or others with whom you're discussing) to share their thoughts. Are there some scriptures that might be meaningful for you to read and discuss?

Why is it important to stay out of debt? Why have so many called debt bondage?

What is a step you can take, individually or as a family, that would help you to get out of debt and begin saving?

In conclusion, I want to return to President Tanner's message, "Constancy amid Change." He suggested some constants that would help us manage our resources wisely:

Constant 1: Pay an honest tithing. . . .

Constant 2: Live on less than you earn. . . .

The key to spending less than we earn is simple—it is called discipline. Whether early in life or late, we must all eventually learn to discipline ourselves, our appetites, and our economic desires. . . .

Constant 3: Learn to distinguish between needs and wants.

Consumer appetites are manmade. . . . We must learn that sacrifice is a vital part of our eternal discipline. . . .

Constant 4: Develop and live within a budget. . . .

Constant 5: Be honest in all your financial affairs.

The ideal of integrity will never go out of style. It applies to all we do. As leaders and members of the Church, we should be the epitome of integrity. (*Ensign*, June 1982, 4–7)

May we give our best effort to freeing ourselves from whatever bondage might be present in our lives, praying earnestly for the help we need in finding relief and release.

Heavenly Virtues, Deadly Sins

It seems to me I've heard about the "Seven Deadly Sins" my whole life, and very little if anything about any "Heavenly Virtues." Oh, I've heard a lot about "do good and be good," but less about Christlike characteristics with that kind of a "title" on them.

The seven deadly sins, on the other hand, are a common list. And they seem to be a collection of contentment disturbers. No doubt about it. Contentment is not a blessing attached to a single one of them. They are indeed deadly! They all seem to lead to serious consequences if we don't recognize, conquer, and eliminate them.

Can you name some or all of the seven? I'll give you a really big help. I learned a mnemonic device a few years ago that will get you ready in case you're on a quiz show or in a class or just in an informal setting where you might have a chance to shine.

Before I continue with deadly sins, I just want to say that you can have some fun making up your own mnemonics, and you can end up memorizing all kinds of amazing things, like the Great Lakes (HOMES), the counties in Maine, the names of the 1987 Rockettes, the bridges in Paris, the highest mountain ranges in South America . . .

I keep getting off track in this book. My busy brain just won't settle down. I get on a roll and it's way too much fun to stop. But let's get back to deadly sins and the mnemonic to help you remember them. It's PEGLAGS. That helps, doesn't it?

Now that this little word is in your brain, in your memory, you might as well make use of it and show off a little. So name the seven deadly sins: Pride, Envy, Gluttony, Lust, Anger, Greed, and Sloth. PEGLAGS. (You could picture some pirates in your mind and come really close to having all seven.)

All this memorizing doesn't matter that much—I just thought I'd give you some fun tips in case you're ready for a new hobby. But, now that you can remember the seven deadly sins so easily, can you think of ways in which they can prevent or disturb contentment? Have you noticed some cause-and-effect events in your life?

Let's look at each one of the seven:

1. Pride. Oh yes, the big one. Parent and promoter of all the others. The tendency to put ourselves ahead of

others. Becoming vain to the point where we need only our own brilliant, accomplished, amazing self, and we have little if any need for anyone else, including God and the heavenly help He offers. How can I possibly experience contentment and peace if I have to continually make sure I'm number one?

2. Envy. I'm not sure why this one is linked to the color green, but for most of my life I've heard that phrase, "green with envy." Who wants to be green besides the Hulk (or whatever his name is) or the Wicked Witch of the West?

Envy is an absolute destroyer, not just a disturber, of peace and contentment, because when we suffer from it we become obsessed with wanting what others have. It could be their talents, their home, their children, their car, their CD and DVD collection, their job, their yard, their candy cane, or anything else. Another way to look at envy is to remember, "Thou shalt not covet!"

Elder Joseph B. Wirthlin cautioned: "Brothers and Sisters, beware of covetousness. It is one of the great afflictions of these latter days. It creates greed and resentment. Often it leads to bondage, heartbreak, and crushing, grinding debt" ("Earthly Debts, Heavenly Debts," *Ensign,* May 2004, 40).

3. Gluttony. The very word is sort of an adipose kind of word. But it doesn't just relate to food and drink, does it? *Gluttony* is an out-of-control desire to consume more than we need. And, again, it seems like the opposite of

contentment, where we recognize we have enough, and we experience satisfaction. I think it's hard to satisfy a glutton.

4. Lust. This particular sin involves the insatiable craving for the pleasures of the body. To me it connotes shameless, selfish indulgence. First there are lustful thoughts, and they lead to actions. As the Savior taught, "Whosoever looketh on a woman to lust after her hath committed adultery with her already in his heart" (Matthew 5:28).

5. Anger. Anger is fury. It's having a short fuse, as they say (that's the way I've described it in myself as I've worked through the years to control my temper). It's the instant reaction, the inability to count to 2, let alone to 10. There is no pure love in wrath and anger, only selfishness.

6. Greed. This is the desire for worldly things such as material wealth or gain. A person can be consumed by greed. It's a desire to be pampered, materialistic, and enjoy every luxury known to man (or woman).

7. Sloth. Sounds like a big, lumbering animal, shiftless and lazy. And maybe that's what we look like when we're always trying to avoid physical or spiritual work. Sloth is the desire to get something for nothing, with no thought, apparently, as to how destructive that is.

Wherever someone is getting something for nothing, there's someone somewhere else who's getting nothing for something. Sloth leads to the evils of the dole and the curse of idleness. Work and responsibility are a critical part of Heavenly Father's plan.

Elder Alexander B. Morrison gave the following

description of sloth as he spoke of what is wrong with society:

> I believe that the real reason for the crisis of our time is spiritual malaise, an exhaustion of the soul. This spiritual apathy is described by the word *acedia,* a word which comes from the Greek *a* ("not") plus *kedos* ("care")—hence, not caring, boredom, or apathy. In its modern usage *acedia* refers to sloth, one of the Seven Deadly Sins enumerated by Thomas Aquinas in his *Summa Theologiae.*
>
> But *acedia* signifies more than just spiritual laziness or even indifference. It connotes misplaced priorities, a darkening of the soul, a hatred of the good, a death of the heart. It leads to spiritual paralysis, leaving its victims "past feeling" (1 Ne. 17:45). ("A Caring Community: Goodness in Action," *Ensign,* February 1999, 16)

There they are. All seven. Has it made you itch and squirm just to read about them? None of these deadly sins seem at all inclined to turn us into visual aids for qualities such as self-control or self-discipline, and they certainly don't seem inclined to help us to have enough, to be satisfied and contented.

Mohandas Gandhi had his own way of listing seven traits that he considered to be the most spiritually perilous to humanity. Former U.S. President Jimmy Carter apparently found these (called "The Seven Sins") engraved on the wall of Gandhi's memorial during a trip to India.

Here is Gandhi's thought-provoking list (don't read it too fast; stop and think as you're reading if you have time):

Wealth without Work

Pleasure without Conscience

Science without Humanity

Knowledge without Character

Politics without Principle

Commerce without Morality

Worship without Sacrifice

(*Public Papers of the Presidents of the United States: Jimmy Carter,* 1978, book 1, p. 80)

Let's leave the sins now and turn to the Heavenly Virtues. You might take a minute to write down some qualities you feel would belong on a list like this—a list of heavenly virtues. I think you'd find it interesting to see what comes to your mind.

My first attempt to make a list of seven heavenly virtues ended up with fifteen: Charity, Gratitude, Mercy, Hope, Faith, Joy, Obedience, Humility, Generosity, Simplicity, Peace, Consecration, Optimism, Trust, and Sacrifice. I could have kept adding more, like Compassion, Work, Meekness, and of course Contentment, but I figured I'd stop at fifteen.

I've found some other lists of heavenly virtues that all seem to me to be sources of peace and contentment. For example, in Matthew 25:34–40, Jesus taught us to feed the hungry, give something to drink to those who are thirsty, clothe the naked, visit the sick and the imprisoned, and to be kind to strangers.

In the hymn "More Holiness Give Me" (*Hymns*, no. 131) there are some wonderful suggestions for becoming more like the Savior. Holiness, patience, faith, joy in service, gratitude, meekness, purity, and other heavenly virtues are included.

King Benjamin offered quite a list when he invited his people to put off the natural man, yield to the enticings of the Holy Spirit, become saints through the Atonement, and become as children. He listed qualities to help in this goal, asking his people to be submissive, meek, humble, patient, full of love, and willing to submit (see Mosiah 3:19).

So far, I've not found any indication that someone has gone through the seven deadly sins and tried to come up with an opposite for each one. I thought it might be an interesting exercise to create a list of heavenly virtues out of those seven opposites.

Some would seem obvious, such as humility as the opposite of pride. Some may seem to need a couple of words, like chastity and purity as the opposite of lust, or abstinence and moderation as the opposite of gluttony. Patience could be the opposite of anger, generosity the opposite of greed, work the opposite of sloth, and satisfaction the opposite of envy.

These particular heavenly virtues suggest ways to counteract their corresponding deadly sins. With pride, for example, there are awful consequences, while with humility, there come many blessings. I'll just include one example, "Be thou humble; and the Lord thy God shall lead thee by the hand, and give thee answer to thy prayers" (D&C 112:10). This isn't a "material" blessing, but it is an incredible blessing!

Our conscious effort to develop heavenly virtues helps create a protection against falling or slipping into the deadly sins. We can *replace* a deadly sin with a heavenly virtue. A weakness can become a strength and a source of much happiness and enjoyment.

Let me illustrate by including here something my niece Wendy Sue shared with me. She wrote about the ongoing struggle she had experienced in trying to develop more patience, worried that her frustrations would spill over into the life of her daughter, Sora. She said:

> I slowly grew the ability to step back from a frustrating situation and pray for help. At first it was all I could do just to think when I got frustrated. I would usually just blow up with anger and start yelling at Sora. I knew that I needed to do better than that. She did not deserve an angry Mom.
>
> When I started the process of praying to get through my frustrating times, my frustration had become a deeply ingrained habit that I could not seem to kick. My whole body would tense and my breathing became very shallow. This caused me to actually feel lightheaded whenever I got upset, and

my capacity to think was very, very muddled because I was unknowingly depriving myself of oxygen.

. . . Slowly, the prayers became easier. My anger seeped away. My frustration habit was broken and instead of clenching up, I taught myself to relax and breathe deeper as well as pausing for several seconds before reacting.

I am now infinitely better off than I was in January of this year. I do not think I was ever truly content before now because I knew that I had a very serious flaw. Once I developed faith, I had the key to resolve the problem. God can do anything you want Him to do, you just have to be aware of your needs and *know* He has the power to fulfill your needs. . . .

Sora is now a joy to me and I am content being a housewife. Chores are not bad anymore, and Sora is much, much happier and more willing to cooperate if I ask her to do something. When I got rid of my frustration, and my bad habits died the hard death, Sora followed suit!

When I see her so content, it flows both ways. Her joy is contagious. It makes me happy, too.

Wendy's challenge to replace frustration with patience reminds me of the principle of opposition that is taught most clearly in the Book of Mormon. Lehi, in teaching his son Jacob, focused a lot on opposition. He emphasized that "it must needs be, that there is an opposition in all things" (2 Nephi 2:11).

All of Second Nephi, chapter 2, is amazing, but one of

my favorite verses is verse 13, in which Lehi compares opposites, pointing out how critical it is that we have a chance to *choose* (see verse 27 as well):

> And if ye shall say there is no law, ye shall also say there is no sin. If ye shall say there is no sin, ye shall also say there is no righteousness. And if there be no righteousness there be no happiness. And if there be no righteousness nor happiness there be no punishment nor misery. And if these things are not there is no God. And if there is no God we are not, neither the earth; for there could have been no creation of things, neither to act nor to be acted upon; wherefore, all things must have vanished away.

Well, there *is* righteousness, and there *is* happiness, and there *is* a God. And yes, there *is* opposition. I remember being taught from the time I was little that we can't know the sweet without tasting the bitter.

Can you think of experiences in your own life where you have tasted the bitter and thus have been much more aware of the sweetness of the sweet? I love the phrase from the hymn I mentioned earlier, "More Holiness Give Me": *More praise for relief.* Indeed! Can you tell from the experience Wendy shared that her joy was heightened because she had worked so hard to replace impatience with patience?

My friend Lynn said that at some point she had become increasingly aware of her grown children not being very kind to their spouses, and not showing a lot of patience toward family members. She felt they were being too judgmental and negative. She writes:

> I prayed about this for quite some time, asking Father to touch their hearts that they would be open and accepting of others and their situations.
>
> Then, I had an experience with my husband that opened my eyes and I realized that I was the one who was judgmental and negative and impatient. It was a big AH-HA! I since have prayed fervently that Father would help me to be patient and positive and that I would not judge others. I have always said that your characteristics, whether good or bad, are magnified in your children; I don't know why it took so long for me to recognize the source of their actions.
>
> I experimented with my husband a while back. Instead of finding fault, I started to look for the good things he did. Not only did I look for them, but I commented to him about them. Surprisingly, his good actions multiplied. From this I have learned that I feel a sense of contentment when I show gratitude to others, especially my Heavenly Father. A simple "Thank you!" goes a long way. How much better I feel when I put energy into being positive instead of being negative.

Others have expressed similar experiences with working to make a change in a relationship or circumstance or attitude. This conscious desire coupled with effort reminds me of a story I know you've probably heard, about an elderly Native American teaching his grandchildren about life. He said to them:

"A fight is going on inside of me. It is a terrible fight and it is between two wolves. One wolf represents fear, anger, envy, sorrow, regret, greed, arrogance, self-pity, guilt, resentment, inferiority, lies, false pride, superiority, and ego. The other stands for joy, peace, love, hope, sharing, serenity, humility, kindness, benevolence, friendship, empathy, generosity, truth, compassion, and faith. This same fight is going on inside you, and inside every other person, too."

The grandchildren thought about it for a minute, and then one child asked his grandfather, "Which wolf will win?"

The old man replied simply, "The one you feed."

What a great illustration of what we need to focus on, and the difference that effort makes in our lives. Focusing on heavenly virtues brings a whole bunch more contentment, peace, and joy than if we're "feeding" the deadly sins.

For many years I have been interested in the prayer of St. Francis of Assisi. He chose to live a simple life and dedicate himself to serving God. I know you've heard the words of the prayer that is attributed to him. Perhaps you've heard it sung, too. There are several versions, but here's the one I like:

> Lord, make me an instrument of thy peace;
> where there is hatred, let me sow love;

where there is injury, pardon;
where there is doubt, faith;
where there is despair, hope;
where there is darkness, light;
and where there is sadness, joy.
O heavenly Father, grant that I may not so
*   much seek to be consoled as to console;*
to be understood, as to understand;
to be loved, as to love;
for it is in giving that we receive,
it is in pardoning that we are pardoned,
and it is in dying that we are born to eternal
*   life.*

What a wonderful thing—to replace hatred with love, injury with pardon, doubt with faith, despair with hope, darkness with light, sadness with joy. These are beautiful invitations.

A prophet of God stated, "Ye shall clear away the bad according as the good shall grow . . . until the good shall overcome the bad" (Jacob 5:66).

Don't give up if you don't see progress every single hour of every single day. There may be times when you stomp on one or more of the heavenly virtues you're trying to make part of your character and your life. It may be one experience, it may be a whole day, it may even become a season—but there is still, always and forever, hope smiling brightly before you, giving encouragement, beckoning you to come closer to the heavenly help that is waiting, with the arm of mercy extended toward you 24/7.

Maybe the important thing to realize is that you're already doing it. You've been doing it for essentially your whole life—working to be better and to do better, to conquer hate with your love, to overcome despair with hope, and so on. Little by little, perhaps you've worked on one quality or virtue through many years and many experiences, feeling success and feeling opposition, too.

If you feel safe and trusting, share with someone else what you're working on and let them help you, pray with and for you, support you. It's so nice sometimes to be able to say to someone, "I've made some progress!" or, "Guess what happened yesterday!"

Maybe you have gone through some exceedingly difficult challenges in your life when you felt that the sun would never shine again. And when the sun did finally come up, oh the joy and thanksgiving! Or, if you're still in the darkness, for you I share a phrase from hymn number 117, "Come unto Jesus": "His love will find you and gently lead you from darkest night into day."

The Savior offers us the power of the Atonement and His pure love to bring us from the darkness into the light. Even when we go through our deep waters and fiery trials (see hymn number 85, "How Firm a Foundation"), He is right with us, helping us to become sanctified, refined, purified, holy.

With heavenly help we can move from deadly sins to

heavenly virtues, from guilt to peace, from agony to ecstasy, from hate to love, from desperation to hope, from tears of sorrow to tears of relief, from feelings of abandonment to a knowledge of belonging, and from a lack of peace to contentment.

Consider focusing on a deadly sin that you want to replace with a heavenly virtue (with a lot of heavenly help, and perhaps even asking some loved ones to help as well). Consciously work at it, remembering that not all mighty changes in our hearts come quickly. Most are a long, interesting, worthwhile, sometimes frustrating process.

There will be lots of ups and downs, perhaps through many years and many experiences, struggles, and challenges. But we can be always striving, always trying a little harder to be a little better (and some days trying a *lot* harder to be a *lot* better). May you be blessed abundantly!

What About the Children?

I remember my childhood as a time of much contentment and happiness. These were days of outdoor games, sleeping out under the stars (my best friend and I would find a star that we were positive no one else had noticed, and we would give it a name), buying goodies from Mr. Munson's grocery wagon as it came down our street, walking to and from school and church and pretty much every other place or event, eating green apples, going to the Saturday matinee, wandering across the street to watch Uncle Leo turn wood into beautiful things, dragging Main, practicing for the road show, reading, throwing snowballs at cars. Sometimes I've said that the worst thing that ever happened in my school was when one of us accidentally left the lid off our bottle of cinnamon toothpicks.

Lots of things were simpler, for sure. Our phone

number was "34," and my dad's office number was "70."
My best friend Zonie's number was "81J," and Marilyn's
was "81M." When you picked up the phone, someone on
the other end said, "Operator." You could ask for a number, or for what time it was, or for "information please."
How did they know all they knew?

Sometimes I would ask hard questions, just to test
them: "When is the carnival coming?" "Is it going to snow
on my birthday?" "Where does Bambi live now?" "Why
don't we have palm trees here?" "Has anyone called about
fish bait?" "Who's going to be my teacher next year?"
"What should I get my mother for Christmas?" "How
much wood could a woodchuck chuck . . . ?"

When I was growing up we never heard words and
phrases like "www" or "dot com," CD-ROM or video, or
digital anything. There weren't satellites, credit cards, frequent flyer miles, instant pudding (there was pretty much
nothing instant besides consequences for misbehaving),
audio books, computers, time-share condos, malls. Many
new terms have been added to our standard vocabulary
since then: starter home, upwardly mobile, personal bankruptcy, laptop, download, gated community, online shopping, consumer debt, cable.

Maybe I'm pointing out that we were more isolated
then. We didn't have the whole state, nation, and world in
our living room on a TV screen. I love telling people that
we never ever turned on television on Sunday in my home
in my growing-up years. Not once. Sometimes I point out

that we didn't *have* a TV, and other times I just let them be really impressed.

My own happy childhood taught me the great power of family in my life and in the world I grew up in. Years ago I came across an article in *U.S. News and World Report* that had a list of what they called "America's Most Influential Institutions." This was intriguing to me, and I began reading the list, knowing the family would be listed in the #1 spot.

Well, no, TV was listed as #1. Surely the family would be listed as #2, I thought. Wrong again. In fact, I soon discovered that on this list of 18 items, the family didn't even make the list! This caused me to do a lot of serious thinking. I'm convinced we must diligently work to preserve and protect even the basic purposes of the family.

Elder Horacio A. Tenorio spoke in general conference of building a fortress around our family:

> In medieval times, great fortresses were built around castles or cities to protect them from enemy attacks. In the Book of Mormon, the Nephites built fortresses to defend their families against their enemies. We must make of our homes fortresses to protect our families against the constant attacks of the adversary.
>
> I am not suggesting that we isolate ourselves from the world by digging deep moats or constructing barriers several meters high around our homes, but rather that in our family councils, under the

influence of the Spirit, we establish the activities, entertainment, books, friendships, rules, and habits that will constitute our fortresses. ("Let Us Build Fortresses," *Ensign*, November 1994, 23)

So many people with whom I have talked and corresponded have mentioned that contentment is tied closely to family. My nephew Errol tells of a time when he and his dad were sitting in the living room talking:

> There was no TV, no telephone, no distractions of any kind. It had probably been at least six years since we had actually just sat down and talked, because I had been in the army for so long. We were going through his Russian paintings and discussing various things that had happened in our lives, completely new stories that I had never heard before. I wanted it to last so much longer, and I don't think my dad wanted it to end either, but it always gets late and there is always something that has to be done tomorrow, so he went to bed and I went out with friends. I'm not sure what I did with my friends that night, but I'll never forget that talk I had with my dad.

I think many of us who have lost loved ones (not lost them, really, but seen them go on ahead to live on the Other Side) have realized how precious family and friends are to us. My cousin Barbara said: "Contentment comes to me when I reflect on the companionship I enjoyed for forty years with a husband who cherished and loved me.

Eternal contentment can be mine if I am worthy to be reunited with him and my dearly loved family in the presence of my Father in heaven and His Son."

A man named Richard Wong said something so beautiful: "Bless our home, Father, that we cherish the bread before there is none, discover each other before we leave, and enjoy each other for what we are while we have time."

Sometimes we get discouraged because our families aren't perfect. I don't know if there *is* such a thing as a perfect family. I've seen many that seem pretty close, but even then there are some worries and heartaches and dreams that haven't come true. Perhaps there is some question as to whether we should speak at all about an "ideal LDS family," since it does tend to get us comparing and feeling inadequate at times.

But that reminds me of a quote from President Spencer W. Kimball from his powerful address in the general women's meeting in 1978:

> The Church will always hold aloft the banner of happy family life, for we can do no other! Family life is the best method for achieving happiness in this world, and it is a clear pattern given to us from the Lord about what is to be in the next world.
>
> We have no choice, dear sisters, but to continue to hold up the ideal of the Latter-day Saint family. The fact that some do not now have the privilege of living in such a family is not reason enough to stop talking about it. We do discuss family life with

sensitivity, however, realizing that many sisters do not presently have the privilege of belonging or contributing to such a family. But we cannot set aside this standard, because so many other things depend upon it. ("Privileges and Responsibilities of Sisters," *Ensign,* November 1978, 103)

That's one of those quotes where I feel like adding, "Enough said!"

Thinking about happy families brings to mind a couple I've lived across the street from since 1978, Ron and Shirley Graves. I've watched many of the seasons in their lives as they've raised their nine children. They are great, good people, and I thought of how pleased Heavenly Father must be with their lives as I sat watching the picture-taking in the park as they celebrated their fiftieth wedding anniversary a few years ago.

I remember specifics through the years, like when they had the cow that had to be cared for and milked, providing chores for the six boys. I'd hear that cow some mornings and evenings really bellowing, and I'd know the chores had not yet been done.

One of my favorite times was when all the chairs would come out in front on a warm evening, and the visiting would begin. Anyone was welcome to join the happy group.

So far there are forty-two grandchildren. There will be more. And they're planning on about five thousand great-grandchildren (although they don't have any of those yet).

Shirley's only reservation is, "I don't know if I can make that many quilts!"

There are lots of family gatherings, with vehicles up and down in front of their place and beyond. This happens at the end of summer when Ron and Shirley come home from Nauvoo. They're serving an extended mission there, working in Salt Lake to select and train young people for the musical programs during the year, and then going to Nauvoo to help them perform during the summer months.

How does this work—this parenting and other influence on the little people as they are growing and developing? How do we raise good children, which is certainly one of the best ways in which we can have an influence in the world?

I found an interesting article in a *Newsweek* magazine titled "The Power of No" (September 13, 2004). It spoke of the challenge parents have in saying no to all that their children want:

> This generation of parents has always been driven to give their kids every advantage, from Mommy & Me swim classes all the way to that thick envelope from an elite college. But despite their good intentions, too many find themselves raising "wanting machines" who respond like Pavlovian dogs to the marketing behemoth that's aimed right at them.
>
> Even getting what they want doesn't satisfy some kids—they only want more.

. . . It's time to stop the madness and start teaching kids about what's really important—values like hard work, delayed gratification, honesty and compassion.

A lot of ideas came to me as I read and reread that article. I found myself asking, "How do we do that? How do we counteract some of the pervasive influences and temptations surrounding our families and our children?"

Then I realized that I had been waiting for the authors to suggest family prayer, family home evening, family scripture study, family council, Primary and Sunday School, the *Friend* magazine, the *New Era,* general conference, Young Women and Young Men organizations, and on and on.

We have such incredible resources to help us teach our children correct principles so that they can govern themselves! And although there may not be very many "ahhah" moments in the suggestions that follow, there might be some "ah-so" ones where we realize that we're never asked by our prophets to do anything that doesn't in some way help, strengthen, and protect us.

• *Family prayer*

This makes such a difference in a family, particularly in the lives of children. I remember what our family prayers meant to me, and how it made me feel when my parents would pray for me with me listening. "Help her to be nice and kind," they would say, including lots of expressions of praise and love.

I remember one evening when my parents were older—around 92 and 80. I was going by their house to drop off some milk and other things, and, as usual, I just opened the door and called out. I headed to the back porch room where I always would stick things in the fridge. I could hear my dad's voice, and I realized they were praying and hadn't heard me come in. I quieted right down and peeked around the corner into the kitchen. There they sat, unable to kneel anymore, holding hands across the table with Dad praying. That touched me so deeply. Family prayer had been important all our lives, and it hadn't quit being one of the last things our parents did each evening.

Don't neglect this source of power, protection, comfort, and example for you or your family. This can be one of the most unifying things you ever do.

• *Family home evening*

We had "home night" from the time I can remember as a tiny little girl. Eventually we began calling it "family home evening." We'd have it once a week, and even though there were times when I wasn't too thrilled about participating, I know it made a difference for me and for our family.

This is a time when parents can help children gain a foundation of righteousness. They can learn to feel and express love for each other, for Heavenly Father and the Savior. They can learn important lessons about how to live a good and happy life along the straight and narrow path. I firmly believe that this is one of the valuable tools in helping protect children and families from temptation and harm.

• *Family scripture study*

I think there are some unexpected blessings that come as families read scriptures together, particularly the Book of Mormon. For example, some have even reported that their young children, through participating in reading aloud, have expanded their vocabulary and understanding of language.

Many have said that although it's challenging to gather the family every single day for scripture study, it helps to have family members share with each other what they've been learning in their personal scripture study, and in seminary, Primary, and other class settings. Some families say it helps to have different family members take charge of scripture study on different days.

Many a parent could tell of having a child write home from college or the mission field to say that he or she really *was* listening and really *did* learn things that have been helpful.

President Marion G. Romney said the following about the importance of reading the Book of Mormon:

> If we would avoid adopting the evils of the world, we must pursue a course which will daily feed our minds with and call them back to the things of the Spirit. I know of no better way to do this than by reading the Book of Mormon. . . .
>
> I feel certain that if, in our homes, parents will

read from the Book of Mormon prayerfully and reg-
ularly, both by themselves and with their children,
the spirit of that great book will come to permeate
our homes and all who dwell therein. The spirit of
reverence will increase; mutual respect and consideration for each other will grow. The spirit of contention will depart. Parents will counsel their children in greater love and wisdom. Children will be
more responsive and submissive to that counsel.
Righteousness will increase. Faith, hope, and
charity—the pure love of Christ—will abound in our
homes and lives, bringing in their wake peace, joy,
and happiness. (In Conference Report, April 1960,
110–13)

• *Family council*

This is another tool that has kept coming to my mind
as I've read many, many articles about how to help children
avoid materialism and find contentment. Lessons can be
given in family home evening, and then family council is
a setting where we can discuss together—counsel
together—on all the important aspects of life, making decisions together *as a family* in matters affecting all of us.

President Spencer W. Kimball said of family council:

Children participate in family council. Concerning the governing of our families, we have been
correctly taught that the family council is the most
basic council of the Church. Under the direction of
the father and mother, who should also counsel

together, family councils may discuss family matters, discuss family finances, make plans, and support and strengthen family members. The Brethren have stated that "an atmosphere of listening, honest communication, and respect for the opinions and feelings of others is vital to the success of these meetings." (*The Teachings of Spencer W. Kimball* [Salt Lake City: Bookcraft, 1982], 343)

Imagine the difference it makes when all family members participate in decision making! What a sense of belonging and responsibility. What a wonderful way to help unify a family. I know there are some decisions that aren't "negotiable"—parents need to carefully decide what things the family *can* vote on. Do you trust your children to help decide what time is a good time to be home each evening, for example? Can they help decide who does which chores and how to rotate them? Can they add to a discussion on how to bring more peace into the home and less contention?

I think family council can become an exceptional tool for helping children learn a myriad of skills and abilities. The more significant their input, the more seriously they are likely to take this council opportunity. They learn important lessons such as consequences to choices, and the impact their behavior might have on others. They learn how it feels to be respected, appreciated, and listened to, and they learn to do the same for others.

• *Helping children feel and recognize the Spirit*

Here is a critical ingredient for helping children (and all of us) sort out that which brings peace and contentment from that which doesn't. There are many things you can do to establish a climate where the Spirit can be present, and then to help family members recognize how that feels and learn to respond.

Remember the wonderful list from Galatians 5:22–23 about the gifts of the Spirit: "But the fruit of the Spirit is love, joy, peace, longsuffering, gentleness, goodness, faith, meekness, temperance . . ."

One way to help children recognize the Spirit is to ask them about experiences where you believe they have probably felt the influence of the Holy Ghost. "How did you feel?" "Do you know what that feeling is?"

• *Love*

I remember a funeral for a little two-year-old boy named Andrew on the first day of spring many years ago. One of the many things that touched me during the service was when his parents spoke, and both said, "He was happy while he was with us. He knew that he was loved." *How many children really know that?*

How do you help your children know they are loved? Don't make them guess or wonder. Tell them. Show them. Has it been a while since you genuinely expressed your love to one or more of your children? Remember, too, that tender expressions of love and affection are the opportunity and responsibility of both parents.

• *Service*

In an *Ensign* article, Annette Bowen shared a great idea that had helped her children experience a more meaningful Christmas. As she watched her sons fight over the toys in the pages of a catalog, she wished she could teach them a more giving spirit. The idea came to her as she was putting up Christmas decorations and came upon the fabric advent calendar with twenty-four small pockets. She writes:

> When I filled the pockets with ornaments to be pinned, one a day, to the tree, I added twenty-four different instructions for good deeds. These included "Hug everyone in the family," "Bake cookies and give them all away," "Invite a friend to visit the community manger scene with us," and "Do a secret service for someone."
>
> As a result, we had the best December ever. The children looked forward to each day's suggestion. Soon their friends joined them after school to see what they could do that day.
>
> We learned, as we counted the days to Christmas, to make each day count. ("How Many More Good Deeds until Christmas?" *Ensign*, December 1988, 64)

My friend Karen shared an experience she had with her cousin Holly when they were watching three little boys, all about age eleven, including Karen's brother. She said she and Holly decided to have a family home evening for the boys. This led to the idea of a "Service War."

The rules were simple:

1. It would last for twenty-four hours, from midnight to midnight.

2. There were points attached to each act of service. You got double points for being creative. You lost half the points if you got caught.

3. You lost points if you did anything mean.

They wrote a note to the boys: "One, Two, Three, Four, We Declare a Service War!" and the game was on. All kinds of wonderful things happened, including the boys leaving a note that Karen should go look at her car. They had washed it in the middle of the night! Holly and Karen fixed breakfast and had cut-out footprints leading the boys outside to eat. Kind service went back and forth all day long.

Later on, the boys each wrote a note on a three-by-five card, expressing what they had learned from this day of service. That was the most touching part of the whole experience. "We had no idea how great it would be or what we would teach them through this," reported Karen. "We just thought it sounded fun."

• *Keep the Sabbath day holy*

Our observance of the Sabbath is an indication of our feelings toward and relationship with our Heavenly Father. What are your ideas for keeping the Sabbath day holy? What has worked for you? One thing I've already suggested is making it a part of family council discussion and decisions. We need more ideas of what "to do" to go along with all the "don't do" or "can't do" things.

When I worked as a nurse, I used to try to make Sunday a different kind of day even when I had to be at work. I would work hard on Saturday to clean cupboards and perform other physical labors. I'd polish my shoes, make sure I had a clean, ironed uniform, and have everything ready so I didn't have to do those things on Sunday. Then, on the Sabbath, I'd hum hymns, do extra things for patients, and so on. I know I picked up the notion of making it a different day because of the way I was raised and taught.

President Spencer W. Kimball shared a variety of ideas for things we might do on the Sabbath:

> As we plan our Sunday activities, we may want to set aside time for our family to be together, for personal study and meditation, and for service to others. We might want to read the scriptures, conference reports, and Church publications; study the lives and teachings of the prophets; prepare Church lessons and other Church assignments; write in journals; pray and meditate; write to or visit relatives and friends; write to missionaries; enjoy uplifting music; have family gospel instruction; hold family council meetings; build husband and wife relationships; read with a child; do genealogical research, including the four-generation program and family or personal histories; sing Church hymns; read uplifting literature;

develop our appreciation for the cultural arts; plan family home evening study and activities; plan other family activities; friendship nonmembers; fellowship neighbors; visit the sick, the aged, and the lonely; hold interviews with family members. (*The Teachings of Spencer W. Kimball* [Salt Lake City: Bookcraft, 1982], 217)

• *Be wise in choices of TV, movies, games, music, and other entertainment*

Elder Joseph B. Wirthlin, in a powerful general conference message, spoke of a "word of wisdom for the mind":

The windows of computer monitors and television screens can bring to us very useful information, but they can also bring information that is evil, degrading, and destructive.

The Lord has warned repeatedly against the evils and designs of conspiring men in our day who would enslave us to our appetites and passions by tempting and tantalizing us with obscene images, words, and music. Through his servants the Lord has cautioned us strongly not to take into our minds thoughts that can harm our spirits.

Since 1950, Church leaders speaking in general conference have counseled us some seventy-five times against unhealthy media consumption. In recent years, as standards of public decency and morality have declined and as public media have reflected and often led that decline, these words of loving concern from inspired shepherds of the Lord's flock have come with more frequency and greater urgency. The watchmen on the tower have raised a warning voice.

. . . Just as we exercise great care about what we take into our bodies through our mouths, we should exert a similar vigilance about what we take into our minds through our eyes and ears. ("Windows of Light and Truth," *Ensign*, November 1995, 76–77)

If we are striving for peace, joy, and contentment, but are spending time with violence, immorality, materialism, and all else that is so prevalent in the various forms of media, what effect might that have on our families?

In his *Ensign* article "What's on TV Tonight?" Larry Tucker shares some questions that might be good for a family council discussion as you and your children (as they're old enough to participate) discuss guidelines for TV watching in your home and family:

1. What else could we be doing that would be more constructive and unifying for our family?

2. What are the underlying messages of this program?

3. Are principles contrary to the gospel taught in this program—perhaps subtly?

4. Do the characters dress immodestly or behave immorally?

5. Would we feel comfortable during the entire

program if the Savior was watching with us? ("What's on TV Tonight?" *Ensign*, February 1988, 21)

• *Teach your children about work*
President David O. McKay, who wrote and spoke much about families, said this about children and work:

> When our children are given us, and that admonition "Suffer them to come back to me" is given, three means of developing them are at hand: The first is home influence; the second, activities—avenues of action, including vocations and avocations; and third, social environment. In all three of these there must be the predominating element of salvation—I mean physically, intellectually, spiritually. And what is it? Work! Work in the home! Work; legitimate work, in the avenues of life! Work, legitimate work in the social world! (*Gospel Ideals* [Salt Lake City: Improvement Era, 1963], 479)

Elder Neal A. Maxwell asked if we could afford a society "in which we do not believe in the principle of work? . . . Work is a spiritual necessity, even if it is not an economic necessity, which it is" ("The Prohibitive Costs of a Value-free Society," *Ensign*, October 1978, 54).

Many parents have their children take responsibility and perform chores as soon as possible. Even little ones can have work to do. Many parents have their children add doing their own laundry to their other household chores when they turn twelve or so.

Mary Kirk, in a talk in the BYU Women's Conference in May 1996, shared something about teaching her children to work. She was imagining that the Savior was visiting their home, and she said this to Him:

> Now, come in the kitchen and see the dirty dishes. My firstborn son, with us fourteen years now, is on dishes this week. He's not at all sure that he should have to take a turn doing the dishes, but we're trying to teach him responsibility and self-sufficiency. We need him to be a contributing member of our family and of the community and the world around him. So, he just gets to take part in it the same as the rest of us. I know, I could have done the work for him—that would be easier in a way—but how would he learn? ("Finding Holiness in Everyday Life," in *The Best of Women's Conference, Selected Talks from 25 Years of BYU Women's Conferences* [Salt Lake City: Deseret Book, 2000], 280–83)

• *Create a haven*

There are lots of things we can do to make our homes places of peace, havens where contentment is felt readily and where family members feel safe and loved.

My friend Angie said that she creates a good atmosphere in her home and life by having "pictures of Christ, my family, and 'churchy' (the lamb and the lion) photos in my home. I also like to listen to Primary songs. I'm in the Primary presidency so I listen to the CD that has the sharing time songs for that current year. It helps me learn the songs that will be sung for the program, and I like it when I wake up in the morning with church songs in my mind."

President Marion G. Romney wrote: "Training our children is the best antidote to the materialism, irreverent secularism, declining morality, adult and juvenile delinquency, increasing crime, and general disregard for the laws of God and the dignity of man that so plague our present world. . . . The Church can and will assist parents in training their children. But it can only assist. The Church is not and cannot be a substitute for parents in their most urgent parental responsibility, which according to the Lord is to teach their children 'to understand the doctrein of repentance, faith in Christ the Son of the living God, and of baptism and the gift of the Holy Ghost by the laying on of the hands, when eight years old.' (D&C 68:25)" ("Let Us Set in Order Our Own Houses," *Ensign,* January 1985, 3–4).

As usual, the scriptures give us the clearest guidance available on this issue: "And we talk of Christ, we rejoice in Christ, we preach of Christ, we prophesy of Christ . . . that our children may know to what source they may look" (2 Nephi 25:26). "Train up a child in the way he should go: and when he is old, he will not depart from it" (Proverbs 22:6). May you be blessed in your responsibilities and joys as you—as all of us—interact with Heavenly Father's children.

Simple Gifts

On a Saturday morning in May 1991, I was teaching a workshop in Pittsburgh, Pennsylvania, on simplifying our lives. As a part of that workshop, I shared the words to the song "Simple Gifts." Perhaps you have heard or sung this beautiful Shaker hymn. Here are the words as I found them when I first discovered the song:

> 'Tis the gift to be simple, 'Tis the gift to be free
> 'Tis the gift to come down where we ought to be
> And when we find ourselves in the place just right
> 'Twill be in the valley of love and delight.
>
> 'Tis the gift to be gentle, 'Tis the gift to be fair
> 'Tis the gift to wake and breathe the morning air.
> And ev'ry day to walk in the path we choose
> 'Tis the gift that we pray we may ne'er come to lose.

'Tis the gift to be loving, 'Tis the best gift of all
Like a quiet rain it blesses where it falls;
And if we have the gift we will truly believe
'Tis better to give than it is to receive.

CHORUS:

When true simplicity is gained,
To bow and to bend we shan't be ashamed;
To turn, turn, will be our delight,
Till by turning, turning, we come out right.
(*Joseph Brackett, Jr., 1848*)

As I shared those words on that beautiful May morning in Pennsylvania, I noticed a woman on about the third row who was weeping a lot. I had never met her before, and I wondered what was going on.

That was the first time I met Mary Kirk. She came up after the presentation, hardly able to talk because of the tears, but she managed to explain that she used to be a Quaker, and the song "Simple Gifts" had special significance for her. She had sung it all her life and loved it even more than I did.

Later that morning I met Mary's husband, Jim. They met while attending the same Quaker high school in Ohio. Mary eventually joined the Church and served a mission; Jim was baptized after they had been married for a couple of years. We have been friends for many years now, and I love hearing them speak of their Quaker upbringing. They both say that they brought much of their conservative

Quaker backgrounds with them when they joined the Church. Quakers are called "Friends," short for "The Religious Society of Friends."

They have taught me how tolerant and accepting the Quakers have been, in their experience. They respect others' right to think, act, and worship as they please, and they consider all men their brothers. The family is very important to them, as is the body. (As Mary and Jim have said, "They really live the Word of Wisdom!")

"Friends" are inclined to do deep, reflective thinking. They relish the chance to worship in silence often. They tend to be very frugal, avoiding waste, and they consciously refrain from vanity. They are not so much in a hurry and so busy as the rest of us. Don't you think it sounds as if they've found a way to be more content than many of us?

I remember at the BYU Women's Conference in May of 1996 when Mary Kirk spoke on "Finding Holiness in Everyday Life." She shared in such a powerful, beautiful way. Here are just a few excerpts from her message:

> Christ always said, "Come unto me." But if I want to understand and know the Savior, I have to say to him, "Come unto me. Visit me in my house, in my space on earth. . . ."
>
> I have a good imagination, so I can see the Savior coming up the steps . . . and gently knocking on my door, wanting to come in and bring some peace and

joy to my whirlwind. And I can see myself flinging that door open and saying, "Please, Savior, come in."

This is how I remember Christ and his atonement in my everyday life. I visualize him being here with me. . . .

Mary then describes telling the Savior about all that surrounds her, telling Him about her days and reminding Him of special experiences in her life.

See this spilled dirt? My three-year-old, Logan, and I were planting some seeds the other day, trying to get a head start on the garden. We really enjoy the earth that Thou has given to us, and we think dirt is fascinating. When we come Home, wilt Thou teach us how this works—this dirt, these seeds, and this water? How does it work? . . .

Later she writes:

He teaches me as we go. I'm finally seeing that what I thought was mundane and bothersome is really meaningful and beautiful. And you can, too. Your circumstances and work may be very different from mine, but you can find holiness in them. . . . The mere fact that we are alive today is holy in itself. ("Finding Holiness in Everyday Life," in *The Best of Women's Conference, Selected Talks from 25 Years of BYU Women's Conferences* [Salt Lake City: Deseret Book, 2000], 280–83)

The two rugs in my living room, which Mary wove for me, are reminders of friends who have a lot of important things figured out. Life is about simple gifts—the ones we give, and the ones we receive.

It is a gift to be simple, to figure out what a difference it makes in our lives as we simplify, simplify, simplify. Somewhere in my house I have a bumper sticker that reads, "Live simply that others may simply live." I've not been very good at following the counsel, but I know I'm making progress.

President James E. Faust gave some wonderful counsel in a general Young Women's meeting:

> Women today are encouraged by some to have it all: money, travel, marriage, motherhood, and separate careers in the world. For women, the important ingredients for happiness are to forge an identity, serve the Lord, get an education, develop your talents, serve your family, and if possible to have a family of your own.
>
> However, you cannot do all these things well at the same time. . . . You cannot be a 100-percent wife, a 100-percent mother, a 100-percent Church worker, a 100-percent career person, and a 100-percent public-service person at the same time. How can all of these roles be coordinated? I suggest that you can have it sequentially.
>
> Sequentially is a big word meaning to do things one at a time at different times. The book of Ecclesiastes says: "To every thing there is a season, and a

time to every purpose under . . . heaven" (Eccl. 3:1). ("How Near to the Angels," *Ensign*, May 1998, 96)

Maybe part of living more simply means we're more patient with the sequence of the events unfolding in our lives!

Sometimes I've heard people talk only about "de-junking" when they're talking of simplifying. I know that's part of it, but I'm not just talking about getting rid of *junk*. Sometimes I have to let go of things that have been precious. I like the idea of giving meaningful things away while I can still explain to someone why they're precious.

I visited with several friends and family members to find out what they do to simplify their lives. Here are some of their great ideas:

• Jacque and Don learned a trick years ago. They measure things in "UPLs" (pronounced "U-Pulls"), defined as "units of pleasure." In their words: "That means that no matter what something costs—a lot or a little—the important thing is how it contributes to your quality of life. A very inexpensive item may bring you a lot of joy— or lots of UPLs—while something else may have no emotional or physical value to you, and, consequently, no UPLs. Get rid of it!"

This has me going around my house analyzing things and giving them a "UPL" rating. Fun! And helpful, too.

• Mindy said one of her missionary companions had heard a good idea about how to go through each drawer and *throw* away one-third, *give* away one-third, and *containerize* (that's Mindy's word) the last third. You could try that with closets and boxes, too. And storage units? Maybe.

• Debi said we should cut down on wasted food storage and the space it takes up by only storing what we will really eat. "No more turnip greens," she says. "Yes to six cases of M&Ms, a case of Worcestershire sauce, etc." She said it helped her feel better over the holidays to stop sending so many Christmas cards, and to scale down the decorations.

The fact is that we each find our own way to simplify and enjoy. For me, it really does help to cut down on the decorations. But oh, how I appreciate my friend Russ, who, with help from his elves, including Brenda and Carma, puts together one of the most magnificent villages at Christmastime that I have ever seen.

• Lynn said it has helped her to schedule a time to do the things that wait, such as cleaning out closets. She calendared a Saturday to do that (and said she had to look months ahead to find one) and actually found herself looking forward to that day.

• Cynthia reminded me of my own suggestion to take a picture of the things that are hard to give away, and then she added another idea: "Write in your journal about the event or experience evoked by the object and the feelings and understandings attached to it. Then take a picture and give the item away."

• Glenda admitted what I think many of us feel: we

have too much stuff. She said that for her, clutter is "a visual distraction to our spiritual well-being. When my home is tidy and clutter-free, I can focus on the important things in life, not on what I need to do to clean."

What she said about clutter being a visual distraction to our spiritual well-being rings true to me. I have a room I call my "Christmas Room" (because that's where I keep the wrapping paper and gifts and such), which always turns into the "catch-all" place. About twice a year I can't stand it anymore, and I get in and really clean and organize it. And then I have to keep looking in there, because it looks so good!

Does this happen to you too? Do you sometimes get a closet or cupboard or a whole room cleaned up and you have to keep going back to have a look? I think it might be because an organized spot helps us feel that our lives (not just our closets, cupboards, drawers, rooms, basements, garages, or sheds) are getting less cluttered. And thus our minds are free to do other important thinking, our spirits are able to focus on our top priorities, and our hearts are in the right place—with our best treasures.

My youngest sister, Ann, has taught me a lot about "Feng Shui" (pronounced "fung shway"), which is about getting rid of clutter and getting better organized, more orderly. I looked up the term on Google, and there were no fewer than 1,350,000 responses! It's kind of an oxymoron to have that many places to go to find out how to simplify, isn't it?

Feng Shui, which literally translates from Chinese as "wind and water," is a system for analyzing and altering the flow of energy ("chi") in any environment so that we promote happiness, good health, and other positive feelings in our lives.

While I was working on this book, an interesting thing happened. I was not thinking about Feng Shui or anything, but for some reason it occurred to me one day that all the clutter I had created in the room where I keep my computer was distracting as I tried to write about contentment and "stuff and things" and all.

I recognized from even this seemingly small experience that order *does* tend toward peace and rest and clear thinking. Quite a revelation for the busy brain! I took some time and uncluttered at least part of the room (it's going to take a year to complete all of my projects), and it definitely made a difference for me.

I'll confess, I often find myself whining out my excuses for not getting things done. One of my favorite tactics is to come home after a day or a week or longer and call out in a whiny voice, "Why doesn't anyone ever *do* anything around here?" (I live alone, so you can hear the other part of me starting to laugh.) In fact, when I catch myself whining it almost always makes me laugh—and then I get ticked off because the whining part of me does not appreciate being mocked. I'm not a graceful, pretty whiner. No . . . that would not be MEE. I'm pitiful, and that's why it makes me laugh.

But whining doesn't get me anywhere I want to go. Among the junk I'm trying to throw out of my life, I want to eliminate any tendencies to complain, compare, or criticize.

And so I go back to the beautiful hymn "Simple Gifts," and to some of the reasons I love the words so much. The verses and chorus are so rich with meaning and ideas.

'Tis the gift to be free. Simplicity *is* part of freedom, isn't it? As Mother Teresa said, our "muchness" can be smothering. She's right. And our clutter can be overwhelming.

'Tis the gift to come down where we ought to be. Perhaps this is a call to get off our personal Rameumptom and "come on down!" A call to humble ourselves and not be such show-offs and big-shots. Be gentle, be fair. Be grateful to wake up and breathe the morning air.

And *when true simplicity is gained,* we won't be too proud or stiff-necked to bow and bend. We will be willing to turn, to change, until we come out right.

'Tis the gift to be loving, to be like a quiet rain, blessing others without needing a lot of attention or thanks. That image reminds me of a little song I learned in Indonesia about the love of a mother toward her child, giving so freely, expecting nothing in return, as the sun illuminates the earth. Sweet.

I hope you'll find some new meaning as you read these words and ponder them. How I love this beautiful Shaker hymn! And by the way, I found on the internet one additional verse. What a blessing it is to feel this way:

'Tis the gift to have friends and a true friend to be,
'Tis the gift to think of others not to only think of "me,"
And when we hear what others really think and really
    feel,
Then we'll all live together with a love that is real.

Gratitude

As years and experience have gone by, I have come to feel that one of the most important ingredients for a happy life—a life of joy, contentment, hope, and peace—is gratitude. Surely gratitude—being thankful, being aware, and expressing appreciation—is one of the most important of all heavenly virtues.

If you want to do a little exercise, see if you can make a list, even a small one, with one column for your *needs* and another column for your *wants*. Put a few things in each column, and then put the list away somewhere. Bring it out again a few months or years down the road and see if anything has changed on those two lists by then.

It may be that nothing will change. Or perhaps you'll change one or two things on the list—switching things from one column to another, or adding some and removing others.

As I've done this exercise many times through the years, I've learned a lot about myself. One of my most recent lists is interesting to me because I started doing extreme opposites. In the "needs" column I put "food," "shelter," and "clothing." In the "wants" column I put "tons of food," "a mansion with a three-car garage," and "a designer wardrobe of the latest fads, styles, and trends, with a walk-in closet." I get carried away, don't I. Maybe I wanted to have some things that were easy to kick off the list so I'd think I was making progress in my quest for contentment and gratitude.

Rather than trying to point fingers and put myself or anyone else in one place on some scale, I suggest that we each consider our own needs and wants, and make our own list. It helps me when I consider what is sufficient for my needs, and also when I work to separate need from greed. I really *can* get very carried away.

President James E. Faust shared this information about our basic needs:

> One of this nation's leading pollsters, Richard Wirthlin, has identified through polls an expression of the basic needs of people in the United States. These needs are self-esteem, peace of mind, and personal contentment. I believe these are needs of God's children everywhere. How can these needs be satisfied? I suggest that behind each of these is the

requirement to establish one's own personal identity as the offspring of God. . . .

The basic needs of mankind identified by Dr. Wirthlin—self-esteem, peace of mind, and personal contentment—can be fully satisfied by faithful obedience to the commandments of God. This is true of any person in any country or culture. ("Heirs to the Kingdom of God," *Ensign*, May 1995, 61–62)

Seeing that we are surrounded by such an abundance of blessings, it seems that gratitude should be one of the easier virtues to cultivate. It's interesting that we have so many reminders in the scriptures, as if Heavenly Father knew we would be inclined to forget too easily. We are commanded to "thank the Lord thy God in all things" (D&C 59:7). And perhaps this is an indication that we even need to thank Him for things which are not necessarily easy and pleasant.

Later in the same section, the Lord indicates that He enjoys blessing us. "And it pleaseth God that he hath given all these things unto man . . ." but then the caution: "And in nothing doth man offend God, or against none is his wrath kindled, save those who confess not his hand in all things, and obey not his commandments" (D&C 59: 20–21).

God is *offended* by "those who confess not his hand in all things, and obey not his commandments." Do we consistently acknowledge the hand of the Lord in all aspects of our lives?

Somehow I've had the feeling that one reason He feels wrath that we don't keep His commandments is not because of what *He* needs, but because He recognizes that some blessings cannot come to us except through our obedience.

One of the most thought-provoking words in the Book of Mormon for me is the word *remember.* I'm not a scholar, but I *am* a searcher, and I love to take a word like this one and go through all the scriptures to see how it's used.

I have found that with the word *remember,* we are almost always being asked to think about *blessings*—those through history, yes, but I think our own blessings as well.

Several times I've flown over "The Plains," about 33,000 or 37,000 feet up, and I've tried to remember what I've learned about the pioneers. I've thought of what it might have been like for those who were right down there, experiencing every rock and flower, and all the dust and mud. I have ancestors who made that trek, and I've read some tender accounts of what it was like for them. And then I've thought how quickly and easily I was shooting across that very area, and what little effort was required for me to do it in a matter of hours.

The remembering helped me to feel *grateful.* It helped me to be thankful instead of muttering about how we were up there for all that time (it must have been at least three hours) with no food, no movie, and chairs that were getting narrower by the minute, and not much leg room . . .

Do you see what I mean? I think *remembering* is a very helpful thing for us to do.

Brigham Young offered this idea:

> We are under the necessity of assembling here from Sabbath to Sabbath, and in Ward meetings, and besides, have to call our solemn assemblies, to teach, talk, pray, sing, and exhort. What for? To keep us in remembrance of our God and our holy religion. Is this custom necessary? Yes; because we are so liable to forget—so prone to wander, that we need to have the Gospel sounded in our ears as much as once, twice, or thrice a week, or, behold, we will turn again to our idols. (*Discourses of Brigham Young,* selected by John A. Widtsoe [Salt Lake City: Deseret Book, 1978], 165)

As Brigham warned, we are all too prone to return to our idols when we fail to remember, to acknowledge our gratitude to the Lord.

Here are some verses we frequently use from the book of Moroni in the Book of Mormon. Read them again, and don't skip anything, please. Sometimes it's easy to "skim" if it's something we've read "a thousand times" (and yes, my mother *has* told me a million times not to exaggerate). Here we go:

> Behold, I would exhort you that when ye shall read these things, if it be wisdom in God that ye should read them, that ye would remember how

merciful the Lord hath been unto the children of men, from the creation of Adam even down until the time that ye shall receive these things, and ponder it in your hearts.

And when ye shall receive these things, I would exhort you that ye would ask God, the Eternal Father, in the name of Christ, if these things are not true; and if ye shall ask with a sincere heart, with real intent, having faith in Christ, he will manifest the truth of it unto you, by the power of the Holy Ghost.

And by the power of the Holy Ghost ye may know the truth of all things. (Moroni 10:3–5)

I want to ask you to consider what is being asked of us as we read this record, this Book of Mormon. Here is what we're asked to do: "Remember how merciful the Lord hath been unto the children of men, from the creation of Adam even down until the time that ye shall receive these things, and ponder it in your hearts."

I know you've thought of this before, but think with me again. We're being asked to remember the Lord's mercy to *all* of Heavenly Father's children, including us ("even down until the time that ye shall receive these things"). He asks that we ponder these things in our hearts.

Then we're invited to ask God if these things are not true—is it not true that He has been merciful and generous to all of us through all time? And if we ask with a sincere heart, and real intent, with faith in Christ, we'll *know* it's true. The Holy Ghost will tell us—remind us—that it's true.

And oh, the gratitude this brings into our hearts! We will realize more fully and deeply that the Book of Mormon really *is* a record that bears witness of God's Holy Son, and of the Atonement, and of how much we are loved and tenderly cared for. Over and over again, those who do their best to be faithful are protected and blessed.

Another example: maybe the commandment "Remember the sabbath day, to keep it holy" (Exodus 20:8) refers to a whole lot more than just remembering, "Oh, yeah . . . it's Sunday today."

When I've prayed only to express thanks to Heavenly Father for all He has shared so generously with me, I realize that part of gratitude *is* being *aware*.

I want to tell you about a lesson I have received from Heavenly Father in answer to many prayers. I'm thinking that part of my struggle with materialism and consecration stems from contrast.

The challenges faced by Heavenly Father's children in other parts of the world (and in my own country and village) are to me not just statistics or information, even with pictures, in some newspaper or magazine. No, when I think of contrast, I think of *people*. I picture *individuals* in my mind and my heart. They are *real*. They have *names*, and I've been in their villages and their homes.

My brother Frank said that his eight children have sometimes wondered why they had to live in such a small home. Why couldn't they live in a much larger one? they wanted to know. Then, on a trip to San Diego, they visited Tijuana, Mexico. There the children saw families living on a hillside in cardboard boxes. Since then, they didn't seem to really mind their "small" home.

I wish I didn't need so much contrast in order to be grateful. I want my gratitude to come from deep inside, not just as a reaction to seeing others who seem to be in more difficult circumstances than I am. Even so, contrast can be a *very* powerful teacher. I've thought sometimes that milk and honey must have sounded, looked, and tasted so good to the camp of Israel after they'd been eating manna for all those years.

Elder Henry B. Eyring pointed out that if we count our blessings with faith, the Holy Ghost will often bring other blessings to mind (see "Remembrance and Gratitude," *Ensign*, November 1989, 13). Maybe you'd have an interesting time trying the "ABC" method of counting blessings. I think this comes to mind because of that old song "A you're adorable, B you're beautiful, C you're a cutie full of charm; D you're delightful and E you're exciting," and so on and on, all through the alphabet, kind of cheating on "X" because they can't think of a word.

If you think it would be valuable to try this (including with your family), don't try to get things in some order of importance or it might spoil the fun. Just talk together about all the things you can think of for which you're thankful that begin with the letter "A": apples, animals,

Africa, aunts, ants, acrobats, artists, anesthesia, Altoids, aerobics, answers, air . . . (I know you're adding to the list).

Then we can move to "B": books, banks, beds, brothers, barns, beauty, bread, babies, birthdays, bananananas (ha), bears . . .

And "C": chocolate, cowboys, camels, canyons, cartoons, Christmas, crayons, cruises, cows, Charlotte, canvas . . .

Well, you've had the idea for quite some time, but I couldn't resist carrying on for a few letters. This may not be an idea that has any appeal for you, but then, on the other hand, maybe it would be fun as an activity in a family home evening or in the car on a long trip. "How many things can we think of beginning with the letter 'X' for which we're thankful?"

Okay, don't start with "X." After X-rays, Xerox machines, and xenophobia, it gets hard. But if you skip around the alphabet there will be less chance for some to move ahead to the next letter instead of focusing on the one at hand.

In expressing gratitude in prayers, it helps to be as specific as you've ever been. Include everything from individual family members (name them one by one), friends, electricity, water . . . think and thank. Then, as you finish, let your heart remind you of some things you forgot. Ask yourself what your life would be like *without* some of the things for which you forgot to thank Him.

My friend Rachael said: "Feeling gratitude for what I already have always tempers my heart during times when I 'look at others with their lands and gold . . . ' and wonder why my house can't be bigger, or my car can't be nicer. I sometimes actually sing 'Count Your Blessings' all the way through, making sure I am in compliance with all three verses!" That's a good idea.

Another friend, Kathy, said that sometimes her thank-you prayers are short but sincere. "It's been a good lesson for me, the past couple of weeks, to see how happy I can be when I think of what I do have, rather than what I do not. I've found myself saying little 'quicky' prayers, like, 'Heavenly Father, don't mean to bother you, but just wanted to tell you, at this moment, how grateful I am for air conditioning!' or 'Heavenly Father, thank you for my cute little dog. She just makes me smile! I'm so lucky,' or 'Heavenly Father, thank you for allowing me to have a car, so I don't have to ride my bike or a bus to work. And P.S., I'm really thankful that it's a cute car, too!'"

One of my dearest friends is Mary Jane Davidson Hawkes. We were companions for nine months on my first mission, and I recognized in her some of the qualities I wanted in my own character. One of these was gratitude. Her son Tim shared some excerpts of a letter she wrote to him in September 1991. Her words are even more impor-tant and poignant now because she left us abruptly and unexpectedly a few years ago, and we miss her so deeply. She wrote:

> Life is very good for me, Tim. I love each child born to us. I have a wonderful husband. The gospel

has filled my life with purpose and joy, and I always have twelve or more things waiting for me to do that I really enjoy doing. I feel so grateful for education, for modern conveniences that have freed me from drudgery, and for the endless beauty of the earth. I hope life is good in the same way for you and for each of your brothers and sisters. I am very glad to be alive and to have lived. I have felt the direction and comfort of the Lord along the way. I have an assurance of truth that carries me through difficulties. What more could life give anyone?

Mary Jane and I used to sing a Primary song together that I've loved teaching to those learning English in places where I've lived and served. It is a first-class thank-you song!

> *Whenever I hear the song of a bird*
> *Or look at the blue, blue sky,*
> *Whenever I feel the rain on my face*
> *Or the wind as it rushes by,*
> *Whenever I touch a velvet rose*
> *Or walk by our lilac tree,*
> *I'm glad that I live in this beautiful world*
> *Heav'nly Father created for me.*
>
> *He gave me my eyes that I might see*
> *The color of butterfly wings.*
> *He gave me my ears that I might hear*
> *The magical sound of things.*
> *He gave me my life, my mind, my heart:*

I thank him rev'rently
For all his creations, of which I'm a part.
Yes, I know Heav'nly Father loves me. ("My
    Heavenly Father Loves Me," *Children's*
    Songbook, 228–29)

I've asked myself a question many times: "When does it happen?" When and why do we stop being grateful for what we have and begin to be dissatisfied and want more than we need, the impossible?

How can we consciously become more thankful for what we *do* have rather than being so often dissatisfied because of what we *don't* have? Do you ever remember a Christmas when you opened a bunch of presents and then looked around for more rather than enjoying what you had received?

I think there are several ways we can reduce the tendency to think of what we don't have. One is to consciously stop the thought as soon as we recognize it, and replace it with gratitude. I'm going to offer a bunch of statements illustrating this, and you can kind of skim over them until you land on one that has relevance for you:

"It's true that I don't look like someone from a magazine cover . . . but I feel good about myself, and I love what I'm doing."

"Okay, so I don't have a new dress for the Easter Parade . . . but I have a great new book I'm going to start reading, and I can't wait."

"No, my husband isn't perfect—oh how I wish he'd be

the one to initiate family prayer and family home evening . . . but he's such a great friend and wonderful provider."

"I hate it when I lose my temper . . . but it doesn't happen nearly as often as it used to. In fact, I think I'll have it completely under control in about eighteen more years."

"Yes, our community really got hit by the hurricanes . . . but we're talking to neighbors we've hardly known until now; we're all in the same (damaged) boat."

"No date again this Friday night . . . but my brother's going to take me to the dance on Saturday."

"I drove the family taxi 123 miles today . . . and I sang a whole bunch of Primary songs, sometimes as a part of a duet or trio; I wish I could offer you a CD—we sounded so good!"

"It's so hard being homebound . . . but thank goodness for a telephone, the internet, the postal system, a doorbell, sun coming through the windows, and some great friends."

"My teenage son acts like he can't stand me at all . . . but he's sure dependable when it comes to breathing; I have never had to remind him to do that even once!"

"I've been so lonely since Fred died . . . but I very much enjoy writing letters to the missionaries from our ward; some of them even write back!"

"I didn't get the laundry done again today . . . but it feels so good to have done three more years of my personal history."

"My team lost their game last night . . . but the sun still came up this morning, and it's a beautiful day."

"This chemo hair loss is a bummer . . . but I've got wigs that have me looking very much like someone you used to have a poster of."

"I can't believe I forgot our anniversary . . . but I did bring her a bouquet of Venus Fly Traps for National Alligator Week."

"It bugs me to death when only eleven women come to Enrichment . . . but we sure have a lot of memorable moments together."

"My baby wakes up several times during the night . . . but we're bonding very well, and I'm reading more in the scriptures than usual."

"It is a fact that I don't have a college degree . . . but I've got the equivalent plus some post-graduate work from the learning that has come to me from my life's experiences."

"While I don't have a beautiful yard . . . I really do have a beautiful dog, and it's kind of sweet the way he's digging up all kinds of imaginary bones."

"Christy will probably never clean her room before she turns twenty, if then . . . but oh how I love to hear her singing in the mornings."

"It's true I don't have many of my own teeth left . . . but it sure cuts down on the cavities."

Are you getting the idea? We really *can* look at a glass as being half-full instead of half-empty, and we truly can change our thoughts from negative to positive much of the time. And for those times when it's just not possible, please hang in and hang on. I've had some of those too. Truly.

One way to practice this with others is to compile a group or family thank-you list. This list can come in handy on those days when you just can't come up with a positive to counterbalance a negative. You could sit together and begin listing blessings, taking turns and going around the circle, round and round, until no one can think of anything else.

Another strategy is to be conscious of the difference in you (and each other) as you steadily, deliberately increase your gratitude and decrease your whining. Watch what happens. Notice differences.

Try this if you feel it would be helpful: Go to a room in your house, apartment, condo, tent—any room—and sit a spell (which I think is the same as "a while"). Just look around and list 10 or 80 things for which you feel grateful. Specific things. You don't need to write them down— just make the list in your head.

I think about what Alma the Younger taught his son Helaman: "When thou risest in the morning let thy heart be full of thanks unto God" (Alma 37:37). This isn't always easy—to wake up in the morning with your heart full of gratitude. At least not for me. But when I do it, it makes all the difference in my day. Actually, I'll admit that I'm a morning person, and I'm usually reasonably cheerful and thankful in the mornings.

One day I was thinking about being grateful for present blessings, and I felt that there are times when I don't thank Heavenly Father for my pennies because I'm sad that I don't have dimes. Is it ever true that we reluctantly let go of one penny, forgetting to thank Heavenly Father for the nine?

I find that when I'm thinking about what I don't have, I tend to get grumpy and crabby. I'm not very pleasant, optimistic, or positive, and I'm no fun to be around. It teaches and reminds me that I can never get enough of what I don't need, actually, because I am *surrounded* with wonderful things. This includes all that is connected to the gospel—light and truth, a knowledge of the Savior and the Atonement, the privilege of communicating with my Heavenly Father, and so on—a *huge* list.

When we focus on blessings, expressing gratitude along the way, we will become increasingly aware of all that has been so generously shared with us. We notice what we're thinking about, don't we?

My friend Sharon told about a friend who did this exercise with her school class:

> She would tell them, "Look around the room and find all the things you can that are purple." After they had a few minutes to do so, she had them close their eyes. Then she said, "Okay, now tell me all the things you saw that were yellow." And they couldn't do it. That's because they had focused so intently on the purple that they didn't even notice the yellow things. She stated it something like this: "That which we

focus on increases. It doesn't really increase, but our perception and awareness of it increases."

Sharon concluded: "You can see the application to contentment and gratitude. When we focus on what we don't have, pretty soon that's all we can see, so we become discontented, and whiny, and unsatisfied. But when we focus on our many amazing blessings, we become more and more aware of them, and thus more and more content and humble and grateful. And I might add, happier. And more peaceful."

President Gordon B. Hinckley pointed out a few things we should notice and remember to be grateful for:

> I feel so profoundly grateful in my heart for the blessings of our Heavenly Father. How good and kind and generous and wonderful He has been to us, as His sons and daughters. How thankful we ought to be every day of our lives for the restoration of the gospel of Jesus Christ, that the God of Heaven and His Beloved Son parted the curtains and opened the work in this, the dispensation of the fulness of times, and brought about a restoration of all previous dispensations. All of the great doctrine, all of the great practices of earlier dispensations in this, the greatest of all dispensations. How thankful we ought to be that somehow the Lord in His kindness and goodness and mercy to us has made it possible for us to enjoy these blessings. ("Latter-day Counsel: Excerpts from Recent Addresses of President Gordon B. Hinckley," *Ensign*, July 1999, 73)

When I think of our abundance, I realize that our Heavenly Father really *does* love to bless us with the good things in life. Maybe you have more because God knows your heart, and he knows you will be grateful and share generously. He also loves to give us those opportunities to share with others, because He knows how much that will help us become more like Him and His Son.

Remember the Poor and Needy

Are you a "have" or a "have not"? This is a question you might ask yourself pertaining to a variety of different categories: Food. Clothing. Shelter. Opportunities. Friends. Memories. Dreams.

I've done quite a bit of thinking about this myself. For instance, with food, I'm a "have." Anyone can look at my size and guess that I've not missed too many meals in my life. Not only do I have plenty, I have extra. And I have so much variety that it's almost overwhelming. I waste too much. (I could have spelled that "w" word another way and it would still be a true statement.)

I'm also a "have" with clothing. If I were to put on even a fraction of the clothing I have in my closet and then somehow get tipped over, I'd never be able to get up. I have too many clothes, and I'm working on cutting down. Simplifying.

When I think of how my shelter got upgraded after the flood of 2000, I recognize that I'm a "have" in my wonderful little home. *Little* is relative, I know. Let's just say it has a one-car garage, an unfinished basement, and no dishwasher. How's that?

But it's truly a palace. I admit it, and I'm so thankful for it. Indoor plumbing. Hot and cold (and safe) running water. Furnace for heating it in the winter, and air conditioning for cooling it in the summer. A refrigerator and a freezer. Cobwebs. Dust.

I'm definitely a "have" in the category of opportunities. When I think of the chances I've had for learning and experiencing, I can hardly believe it. How did this little General from our childhood army games on First West end up with so many interesting opportunities? If you had told me way back then that I would someday live in Africa, I'd have pictured something from the Saturday matinee, and I'd have imagined myself being cooked in a big pot over an open fire!

I know how to read and write, and I love doing both. I've been able to go to school—all the way through college, becoming a nurse. I can use a computer (at a very basic level). I've had the chance to travel and to have friends and mentors in many interesting places.

Am I a "have not" in any category? Of course. I don't have a husband or children. That's a biggie, but I've turned it all over to Someone I trust completely. My job is to keep the commandments, honor the covenants I've made, be a happifier, and respond to the Spirit.

I'm a "have not" in many skills, talents, and experiences. I don't know how to fix things. I don't even know what's wrong, usually. I sometimes talk to inanimate things, thinking they might respond. If the light flickers, I might say, "Quit it!" And maybe it quits, so I think I'm amazing. But then it starts again.

I don't know how to speak Spanish, play the piano, crochet, teach math, fold napkins into animal shapes, sell stuff on eBay, carve things out of wood, fix a leaky faucet, climb cliffs, and so many other things. I'm not a person who knows a lot about birds, although I can tell a seagull from a robin. I know that pineapples and bananas don't grow on trees, but cashews do.

Some days and in some seasons I've been a "have not" in a variety of different categories. So I've been aware most of my life that everyone I meet has something to teach me.

I remember learning a phrase when I was still a little person that went like this: "Bless the poor and the needy, the sick and afflicted, and those who have cause to mourn." I would listen to prayers, and I'd hear that phrase a lot. So when I wanted to be impressive, I'd stick it my prayers too. It wasn't easy to get it all right the first few times I tried. It was like trying "rubber baby buggy bumpers." But gradually it rolled off my tongue, a long time before I knew what all it meant. In fact, I realize that I still may not know—not really. But I want to.

I think I know one source for the phrase. It's from Doctrine and Covenants 52:40: "Remember in all things the poor and the needy, the sick and the afflicted."

What does it mean to *remember,* and more particularly to remember the poor and needy, the sick and afflicted in all things?

Elder Glenn L. Pace said: "It is worthy to note to whom the commandments to take care of the poor were given. My review of the scriptures on this subject suggests to my mind that it is more of an individual responsibility than an institutional one" ("Infinite Needs and Finite Resources," *Ensign,* June 1993, 50).

We get to help. Sometimes we help directly, and sometimes we make contributions that can go to help people we will never meet—at least not while we're earthlings.

And, speaking temporally, who are the poor and needy? If we look at statistics, we can recognize that there is quite a gap between those who have and those who have not. Are we unknowingly pulling away from those who need us? Do we realize how much *we* need *them?*

President Marion G. Romney reminded us that "There is an interdependence between those who have and those who have not. The process of giving exalts the poor and humbles the rich. In the process, both are sanctified" ("The Celestial Nature of Self-Reliance," *Ensign,* November 1982, 93).

There have been many different ways of describing the differences between the rich and poor in this world. I've seen several versions of something called "If the world were a global village." Here is one version:

If we could shrink the earth's population to a village of precisely 100 people, with all the existing human ratios remaining the same, it would look something like the following.

- There would be 57 Asians, 21 Europeans, 14 from the Western Hemisphere, both North and South, and 8 Africans.
- 52 would be female, 48 would be male.
- 70 would be nonwhite, 30 would be white.
- 70 would be non-Christian, 30 would be Christian.
- 6 people would possess 59% of the entire world's wealth, and all 6 would be from the United States.
- 80 would live in substandard housing, 70 would be unable to read, 50 would suffer from malnutrition.
- 1 would be near death; 1 would be near birth; 1 (yes, only 1) would have a college education; and 1 would own a computer.

That's pretty dramatic. In another version of global statistics, it's reported that the real issue is not consumption itself but its patterns and effects. And inequalities in consumption are stark.

Globally, the 20% of the world's people in the highest-income countries account for 86% of total private consumption expenditures, the poorest 20% a minuscule 1.3%.

I remember reading estimates from the United Nations, World Health Organization, and Unicef stating that nearly 42,000 children die *every single day* in this world from *preventable causes,* mostly from diarrhea and the resulting dehydration (see *Deseret News,* December 31, 1982).

And *every single day* here in America, we spend more than a billion dollars on groceries, consume more than 25 billion gallons of water—almost *200 gallons per person*— and throw out close to 2 billion pounds of trash (see *Deseret News,* July 1, 1987). Notice that these numbers are from way back in 1987; I don't have comparative current information.

As President Gordon B. Hinckley has said, "Ours is such a wasteful generation. The disposal of garbage has become one of the great problems of our time. Part of that comes of wasteful extravagance" ("Thou Shalt Not Covet," *Ensign,* March 1990, 5).

What are the implications for us? I think one is a need for gratitude. We are so blessed! Another implication for us might be that we need to see if we can share more generously. As the scriptures invite: "See that ye love one another; cease to be covetous; learn to impart one to another as the gospel requires" (D&C 88:123).

Elder Glenn L. Pace has given this counsel:

> There is a state of human misery below which no Latter-day Saint should descend as long as others are

living in abundance. Can some of us be content living affluent life-styles while others cannot afford the chlorine to purify their water? I struggle constantly with this balance. I believe I have learned a divine truth, however. I cannot become sanctified without serving others, and I will be held accountable if I rob another of the opportunity to give service. ("Infinite Needs and Finite Resources," *Ensign,* June 1993, 54)

Obviously, the poor and the needy would include more than just those who suffer from a lack of physical or temporal resources and blessings. When the Savior described those who needed help, using words like *hungry, thirsty, sick,* and *naked,* He was not just referring to a hunger for food or a thirst for drink.

In the Book of Mormon there is one account of people being poor because they were treated that way. Alma and a wonderful team of missionaries had gone to teach the Zoramites, a group who had dissented from the Nephites. They began to preach, and they had some success among "the poor class of people" (Alma 32:2).

There is a description of some of the reasons as to *why* these people were poor. Read and think. We're in Alma 32:2–4:

> They were cast out of the synagogues because of the coarseness of their apparel—
> Therefore they were not permitted to enter into their synagogues to worship God, being esteemed as filthiness; therefore they were poor; yea, they were

esteemed by their brethren as dross; therefore they were poor as to things of the world; and also they were poor in heart.

. . . because of their poverty as to the things of the world.

Those who first responded to the message of the gospel were poor because they were esteemed by their brethren as dross—they were treated poorly! And they weren't allowed to worship in the synagogues (which they had built with their own hands) because they apparently didn't have nice enough clothing.

In April 1994 I was teaching a class at the Missionary Training Center about how to help people come back who had quit participating in the Church. We talked of many reasons why people go away, and I emphasized that it didn't matter as much how *we* felt about the reason as how *they* felt about why they left. I asked the group why people leave.

One of the missionaries shared something that I'll never forget. She said that while her husband was in the bishopric of their ward, she was advised that it would be best for her not to have a calling but just to spend time with her family and be supportive of her husband. So that's what she did.

When her husband was released from the bishopric, she waited with anticipation for a calling. She was anxious to begin serving in that way again. It didn't come. Time went by and she felt discouraged—she wanted to be involved. Finally, after a lot of time had passed, she decided to go and talk to the bishop. She asked him about it, saying she was wondering if there was some reason she hadn't received any calling. She was ready, willing, and able to serve. His response: "No one has asked for you." Ouch. I remember how it hurt even to *hear* about this. I wasn't the only one who shed some tears.

This dear soul said that if she hadn't been strong, this might have given her enough reason to go away. She thought, "If no one needs me, then why come?" I could tell that even years later it still hurt her.

Sometimes we treat others so poorly that perhaps we add to their own feelings of inadequacy. I remember a classmate my sister Charlotte had when she was in the fifth grade. This little girl was not treated very well, and it showed in her countenance and in the way she responded to others.

But she couldn't resist Charlotte's friendship, and she came to our home a few times. One day, my mother had an idea. It was almost time for the annual "May festival" at school. She helped this little girl get a new dress and some new shoes, and got her hair washed and fixed in an attractive way. It was like a new little person emerged! Even her own teacher didn't recognize her!

There are many different ways to be poor and needy, and there are so many ways in which we can reach out to each other. Many have said that they were taught to be kind to everyone. I certainly was taught that. I remember my parents telling me that in every home there is some sorrow, some burden, something that's hard. And, on the other hand, all people need to give. This is true of affluent Saints and the poorest of the poor. Everyone in every circumstance can offer some kind of help.

Many years ago when I had undergone an extremely challenging experience and had moved home to heal for a while, my little sister Ann, not knowing a lot about what had happened but knowing that I was very sad, would come to my room each evening and read to me from a story about "Good Queen Bess" until I fell asleep. What a tender, compassionate thing for a little sister to do so intuitively.

How about embarking on a scriptural adventure with me. Are you up to it? I'd like to suggest an activity that I think you'll find very revealing. This can be done "solo" or with others, whatever you'd find most meaningful.

If you have someone to read and study with you, it would be helpful if you had two copies of the Book of Mormon available. Open one to Alma 1:25–31, and open the other to Alma 4:6–12.

In the first reference, Alma 1:25–31, there is a description of a time when the people were righteous, they prospered, and they took good care of each other. Watch for specific things about the way they treated each other, and the specific blessings that accompanied their righteousness.

Now, reading Alma 4:6–12, make note of some of the differences in the way the people were treating each other.

Remember that there was only a short time between these two events (which makes this story very sad).

Discuss or write about some of the things that stood out to you. For example, how did people treat each other? These were members of the Church, and they changed so dramatically in such a short time. Can you identify some of the reasons this happened?

How could we guard against slipping into the kind of living described in Alma, chapter 4? How do we avoid becoming filled with pride, setting our hearts on riches and the vain things of the world, looking down on others, being contentious, envying, being poor examples, causing inequality, and turning our backs on those who are hungry, thirsty, sick, and so on? This downslide happened to a whole group of people, but could it also happen to us individually if we're not careful?

One way we guard against slipping into pride and other bad habits is to continue being generous with others, not just with monetary means, but with other resources as well. And it's nice to remember that when we're asked to give, the request is often accompanied by a phrase like "according to that a man hath." In other words, we're not asked to give what we don't have.

In Mosiah 18, we can read of how Alma gathered the people who had been listening to him teach, and he made sure they understood their baptismal covenant. After that, he and all the others were baptized. The rest of the chapter is an explanation of what it means to be covenant people. Read again with me what he teaches in verses 27–29:

> And again Alma commanded that the people of the church should impart of their substance, every one according to that which he had; if he have more abundantly he should impart more abundantly; and of him that had but little, but little should be required; and to him that had not should be given.
>
> And thus they should impart of their substance of their own free will and good desires towards God, and to those priests that stood in need, yea, and to every needy, naked soul.
>
> And this he said unto them, having been commanded of God; and they did walk uprightly before God, imparting to one another both temporally and spiritually according to their needs and their wants.

How gentle God's commands. How kind His precepts are. If we have abundantly, we can give abundantly, and if we have only a little, we give little. And if we don't have anything, others can share with us. Our sharing is to respond to both temporal and spiritual needs and also wants. That's interesting, isn't it.

In a similar vein, King Benjamin taught that to retain a remission of our sins and walk guiltless before God, "I would that ye should impart of your substance to the poor, every man according to that which he hath, such as feeding the hungry, clothing the naked, visiting the sick and administering to their relief, both spiritually and temporally, according to their wants" (Mosiah 4:26).

We're asked to share according to what we have. Our offering is accepted in that spirit—according to what we have. And I love the way equality is described in 2 Corinthians 8:14–15. It does not mean that we're all the same, or that we have an abundance in the same ways at the same times (of the same things).

But when we do have an abundance, it becomes a supply for another's want—it helps those who don't have enough. And then of that which they have in abundance, they also share. That's equality—giving what we can from our abundance. It all belongs to God anyway. He lets us participate because He knows it helps us to become more like Him and His Son.

So we share, from what we have, from our abundance. And, as Alma explained, we give of our own free will and also according to our good desires toward God.

What if we choose not to give? What if we decide to keep everything for ourselves, or we don't recognize the need we have to give? I return to some verses from the Doctrine and Covenants:

> I, the Lord, stretched out the heavens, and built the earth, my very handiwork; and all things therein are mine.
>
> And it is my purpose to provide for my saints, for all things are mine.
>
> But it must needs be done in mine own way; and

behold this is the way that I, the Lord, have decreed
to provide for my saints, that the poor shall be
exalted, in that the rich are made low.

For the earth is full, and there is enough and to
spare. . . .

Therefore, if any man shall take of the abundance
which I have made, and impart not his portion,
according to the law of my gospel, unto the poor and
the needy, he shall, with the wicked, lift up his eyes
in hell, being in torment. (D&C 104:14–18)

Wow. What does that mean? I guess it means what it
says—that if we don't share of the abundance that has been
so freely given to us, we'll be in a world of hurt. One of my
friends once said that "hell is truth seen too late." That's a
chilling definition!

Let's look at one of the parables taught by the Savior
and see if it can tie in to what we just read. This is in Luke
16:19–31. It's the parable of the rich man who had plenty
to eat and terrific clothing to wear. A poor man named
Lazarus was his neighbor and a beggar and just wanted
some crumbs to eat. Lazarus died and was carried by the
angels into Abraham's bosom. The rich man died and was
buried. (It's interesting to me that his name isn't included.)

The first verse I'll share, which is verse 23, sounds a lot
like what we just read in Doctrine and Covenants 104:18:

And in hell he lifted up his eyes, being in tor-
ments, and seeth Abraham afar off, and Lazarus in his
bosom.

And he cried and said, Father Abraham, have mercy on me, and send Lazarus, that he may dip the tip of his finger in water, and cool my tongue; for I am tormented in this flame.

But Abraham said, Son, remember that thou in thy lifetime receivedst thy good things, and likewise Lazarus evil things: but now he is comforted, and thou art tormented.

And beside all this, between us and you there is a great gulf fixed: so that they which would pass from hence to you cannot; neither can they pass to us, that would come from thence.

Well, what do you know—they had traded places! Now the formerly rich man was very thirsty, and Lazarus wasn't. And the rich man wanted Abraham to let Lazarus come and give him just a drop of water from the tip of his finger to cool his tongue. I'm thinking that if he could have done so, Lazarus probably would have. But Abraham explained that it was too late.

It's as if the rich man worked hard during his life to be separated from others—to keep them on their own side of the wall—and when he eventually received what he had desired so much, he found out it wasn't what he wanted at all.

Think with MEE about this verse from the Book of Mormon, in which the Savior is speaking: "And blessed are the meek, for they shall inherit the earth" (3 Nephi 12:5).

Think of it. Might the word *meek* refer to those like Lazarus who don't seem to have much while they live on this earth? The meek shall inherit this earth—the gold, the oil, the diamonds, and all the other things that have been made precious and costly. The meek will also inherit the sunflowers and streams, the mountains and valleys, the tropical rain forests and the amazing deserts. And I guess it would include all the elephants, dogs, whales, birds, and every other beautiful and interesting living thing.

I have met so many in my life who seem to be meek enough to inherit the earth. At first, I would almost automatically describe those I met, first in Asia and eventually in Africa and other places, as "poor." Then why were they so content, and so happy?

I began to recognize that these "poor" were much richer than I in many important ways. So much of what I thought was "the way things were" began to be challenged in some deep and sometimes disturbing (uncomfortable) ways.

Matthew Cowley learned much from his time among the people of the Pacific Islands:

> In unfurnished thatch-roofed huts in the South Seas I have witnessed greater peace of mind, more happiness and contentment, enjoyed by simple natives than exists in too many of the luxuriously appointed mansions of the rich. In the humble native hut man is not existing by bread alone. The words of God play a great part in the program of his living. Each day is commenced by invoking the blessings of heaven upon himself and his family, and at the close of each day

prayers of gratitude are offered for blessings received. (In Conference Report, October 1951, 102)

As far as I can remember, before my first mission in 1962 I hadn't thought much about things like this—about materialism, luxury, or abject poverty. I knew I had more books, clothes, and food than some, and I also knew there were some who had lots more books, clothes, and food than I. But I didn't think much about it.

I especially didn't wonder much about whether there were any implications for me and my life because of my many blessings. Had I somehow been isolated from those who might need me? Did I have an inkling of how much I needed them?

I want to be more aware of others. I want to be more responsive when there's anything I can do. I can't do *every-thing,* but I can certainly do *something.* Maybe there's someone crying for help, and if I'm sensitive to the Spirit I can hear that cry and do a little something to lift a heavy burden.

Glen and Amy, my friends who have ten children, want them to learn the value of service and sharing. They write: "Twice a week we bake bread and cookies as a family and deliver them to our subscribers. The proceeds all go to 'Mothers without Borders.' We know that for every $6 the kids (and parents) earn, another kid in Ethiopia gets a uniform that allows him or her to go to public school." Glen said he felt it was a good thing for all of us to reflect on—that while $6 may not seem like much, it's an awful lot for kids elsewhere.

Some friends told me of a service activity they did as a family. They would make about three dozen lunches every Sunday night. The mother says: "I would buy everything we needed on Friday or Saturday and we'd get an assembly line going with our four or five kids that were home, and away we'd go. I would keep on hand enough sandwich-sized bags, paper bags, mustard, mayo packets, napkins. I'd have room in the refrigerator to keep them, then would deliver them to a local shelter on Monday morning. They loved our lunches! It was a great family activity."

We can reach out to others through our generous donations. President Gordon B. Hinckley said: "I wish we could just expand our humanitarian efforts. This Church is doing a great work, far greater than people realize, in reaching out to people who are not members of the Church across the world. I wish we had more that we could give more" ("Excerpts from Recent Addresses of President Gordon B. Hinckley," *Ensign*, August 1996, 60).

Something wonderful happens when we reach out unselfishly to others in love and kindness. It happens to those whom we help, it happens to us, and it even happens to those who are around us. We are all poor and needy in some ways and rich in others, and we need one another more than we perhaps realize.

What, Then, Shall We Do?

I think I first heard the phrase at the movies: "What, then, shall we do?" It was in the context of some tragic circumstances in the lives of people in what we call a Third World country, and those in a position to help were asked, and were asking, "What then shall we do?"

You might be expecting my response to be something like this: What we must do is give away everything we have, move to a 400-square-foot apartment, and live out our days with two pair of shoes and all our clothing on ten hangers and in one drawer. We must eat half of what we've normally been eating, and all our "stuff and things" should fit in one bag that will fit in the overhead compartment of an airplane.

But surprise! That's *not* what I'm going to suggest. No, no, no. If that's what you were prepared for, I haven't done a very good job of sharing. Hang in there with me, and let's see if I can adequately explain myself.

Through the years, I've had long conversations with myself and in my prayers as to what God wants me to do with the generous blessings He has showered upon me. It has been especially difficult when I've returned from an away-from-home experience and have realized again how much "stuff and things" I've accumulated.

Maybe there have even been times when I've anticipated He would say, "Give away everything you have, move to a 400-square-foot apartment . . ." and so on. But no. Every single time I have asked Him earnestly what He wants me to do, I get the same essential message.

These are the three distinct impressions that always come into my mind and my heart: *enjoy, appreciate,* and *share.* Wow. Think of it! First He invites me to *enjoy.* Isn't that just like a loving Heavenly Father? It's not just *one* of the things He wants me to do, it's the *first* one. Enjoy!

So what then shall we do? Let's *enjoy* our blessings! The more I've thought about it, the more I've realized that I don't do that enough. Do we *enjoy* our days, our families, our opportunities? Do we *enjoy* our food, water, books, freedom, health, and on and on?

This could be big. This could be so important. Can you imagine how frustrating it would be to work hard and have wonderful things and never take the time to enjoy them? This would include not taking time to enjoy our loved ones—our family, our friends, our neighbors. What might we be missing?

Carry it a step further and let's not feel guilty about the wonderful blessings that surround us. Sure, I've been kind of hammering on materialism and having too much stuff and things, but don't let me go overboard. Let's back up and be *happy* with the beautiful, wonderful blessings that have been shared with us by a kind and generous Heavenly Father. Enjoy!

Next, He asks me to *appreciate*. I've decided to have a whole chapter about gratitude, but I'm including it here briefly because it's one of those "What then shall we do?" answers. We shall *appreciate*. We shall thank Him—and others—more adequately, more often, with more awareness.

And the third thing is to *share*. I have found that one of the surest ways to experience contentment is to be generous in sharing with others. One ingredient of contentment is the knowledge that we have done what we could to help others, and in the process we have helped the Savior Himself.

In the context, then, of us being covenant men and women, and knowing something of the wide gap between those who have and those who have not, and knowing of the perils of iniquity and inequality, I do ask myself and others, "What then shall we do?" The following list includes not just my own ideas but many insights from family and friends.

Remember that we're not operating on the assumption that every single idea or suggestion would be magical and ideal for every single reader. Oh, no. But perhaps one or two or more ideas will seem possible and even valuable in your particular circumstances. Maybe this list will have different meanings for you as time goes by and you find yourself in different circumstances, different seasons.

• *Keep doing the wonderful things you're already doing.*

As I've lived a few years and met a lot of people and visited in many homes, I've come to the conclusion that there is so much *goodness* in every single child of God. Your goodness and your generosity make a difference in the world. Keep doing what you're doing.

• *Continue being the best covenant keeper you can be.*

I've known "forever," it seems, that we get better at doing things the longer we do them, and I'm thinking this is true for keeping covenants. For example, the more we seek to bear one another's burdens, to mourn with those who mourn, and to comfort those who need comforting, the more *aware* we become of who needs this kind of help and how to offer that which will make the "best" difference in others' lives.

• *Continue to be faithful in tithes and offerings.*

This not only helps us to remain personally worthy to go to the temple, but our generosity will help make that possible for so many, many others.

Would it be helpful in your family to take some time discussing this topic? Would it help to go over the donation slip and make sure everyone understands what each area of contribution means—where the funds go, how we help others, and the blessings promised to us for our generosity?

I think it makes a difference for most of us, even little people, when we understand more about the "why" of things. Why do we pay tithing? What does it mean to donate a generous fast offering, and where does that money go? Who gets helped when we contribute to ward and general missionary funds, and to the Book of Mormon? What's humanitarian aid? What difference does it make if we contribute to temple construction? What does "perpetual education" mean? (I can hear myself getting nervous when I was younger, thinking this one might mean that I had to go to school forever!)

A few years ago when my niece Mary's daughter Elise was about four years old, she went to the annual tithing settlement with the family. She had a whole dollar to contribute. At some point, the bishop, who just happened to be her uncle, reached for the dollar, and she extended it in his direction but then stopped abruptly and asked, "So what are you going to do with it?" And she waited for an answer before she made her donation.

It's my feeling that as children participate, both with the family and individually, in making whatever contributions they choose, blessings will come. We can all receive unexpected blessings that fill needs we may not have even realized we had!

• *Spend less time and money on things you don't really need.*

This can bring such a sense of freedom! And it's almost like another "get rich quick" scheme. I have learned to say to myself when something in a store looks like it wants me to take it home: "Do I need this?" Most often the answer is, "No, you don't." It helps me to make a list, too, when I go shopping.

Time is also important—it's one of the resources we have that can be shared as well as used. Make appointments with yourself for the things that will make a big difference in your contentment, peace, and general well-being. We're usually better at scheduling our time for everything and everyone besides ourselves.

What would make a difference for you? Going to the temple? Reading the scriptures? Some solitude? A walk? Playing golf or tennis? Taking a class? Playing the piano? Entertaining the neighbors by twirling your baton on the front lawn?

I can almost hear you responding, "Yes, yes, yes," but then telling me I don't understand your situation. You have responsibilities with your family, your work at home or "the office." You haven't had a spare moment since 1993.

What if you were to get a baby-sitter once a month for an afternoon and evening so you could have that time to look forward to, and you could plan whatever you wanted to do? It might be the best thing in the world for you and your spouse or a friend to go to a movie and to dinner. Save your pennies and try something like that.

• *Be careful with food, water, and other resources.*

Sometimes I drink part of a glass of water and just pour the rest down the drain, thinking, "I'm not thirsty enough to finish this." Well, somewhere there is someone who *is* thirsty—very, *very* thirsty. And perhaps as I consciously try to be less wasteful, I can feel the joy of sharing.

I want to admit something. Maybe you'll understand this. When there is an abundance of something, it's easy for me to feel it, and to be less careful about using or keeping only what I need.

For example: During the years Utah had an abundance (that would be "enough and to spare") of heavy winters and the resulting water, I wasn't as careful about using water. My goodness, there was even a *river* running down State Street! I had to go have a look and take a few pictures. I actually walked across a *bridge* on State Street!

It is often more difficult to be careful when we're surrounded by plenty . . . by enough and extra.

• *Avoid the great and spacious building.*

Several years ago I was asked to participate in the BYU Women's Conference and to speak on the topic of materialism. About fifteen minutes before I was to give the talk, some distinct additional thoughts came into my mind. I laughed out loud at this one: "Don't even go *near* the great and spacious building, even if it's in a Parade of Homes!"

The impression I got was that the safer I can be, the farther away I can stay from temptations, the better my life will be.

• *Continue working on having a house of order.*

This isn't easy, is it? I mean, you put down a piece of paper and it grows! Next time you look, there are 12 or 37 things on top of it!

And dust. How does so *much* of it get in? What is my dust teaching me? Perhaps that there are some things that have been unused, undisturbed, in quite a long time—things that have been neglected.

Do relationships get dusty? Are there some that I've neglected? Even the relationship between me and my Heavenly Father? Are there friendships I need to dust off and renew?

• *"Use it up, wear it out, make it do, or do without."*

I've heard that little statement all my life. I think it's something the pioneers came up with. The longer I live, the better I understand it, and the better I like it.

One example for me is my brother Richard's slippers. I love them. I think there is now officially more duct tape on those slippers than original materials. They're incredibly beautiful.

Another saying comes to my mind that isn't exactly the same as "use it up, wear it out . . . ," but that feels similar: "Waste not, want not." Have you heard that one a lot too? I waste too much. Have you had to get an extra garbage can to throw out everything that accumulates in just one week?

- *Slow down!*

I need this advice. I need it pretty much every single day of my life. Slow down!

What good is a full schedule if we can't keep up? Why have I reached a point where I feel guilty if I'm not in a frenzy? Why am I always in such a hurry?

Pretend you're on the highway of life and you come to a construction zone, and there's someone in a bright orange vest smiling at you and holding out his hand, giving the waving gesture for "slow down." And you feel yourself letting up a bit, relaxing your muscles, allowing the tension to slowly slip away. Ah . . .

"Be still" is perhaps a way our kind Heavenly Father tells us to *slow down.* Elder Dallin H. Oaks teaches us that "we should not be so occupied with what is routine and temporal that we fail to cherish those opportunities that are unique and spiritual" ("Spirituality," *Ensign,* November 1985, 61).

We live in a world where there seems to be an effort to keep us busy and occupied every single minute of every single day. We're bombarded with information, gadgets, stuff to read and watch and listen to. . . . Didn't I go to a gas station recently where they had little ads and information for me to peruse while I was filling my car? They're everywhere! Am I incapable of thinking, or of entertaining myself? Am I better off watching a news update at an ATM than using the time to just *think?*

Are all of our gadgets preventing us from noticing what's going on around us, and who's around us? Are we missing some of the magic of serendipity in our lives because we're so busy, so preoccupied, so smothered in our stuff and things? Where are the moments in our day for inspiration, for good ideas popping into our heads?

Do you remember that bumper sticker from years ago: "Stop the world! I want to get off!" Perhaps living in the fast lane is like an addiction. We don't want any "speed limits" in our lives.

What are the antidotes to speed and busyness? Are there any? Maybe the "two birds with one stone" idea will help (although I'd like a better way to express it . . . who wants to kill two birds with a stone!). Could we listen to the scriptures and other good books, or reruns of past general conference talks, or music, as we're walking, working, riding on the bus, waiting for someone? Could we include someone we need and want to talk to in our exercise routine or other activities?

What has happened to our holy days, our days for contemplation and rest? Do we ever find a way to keep the Sabbath day holy, wholly? And if we feel we're wasting time in having a day of rest, where have we gotten so far off track? Maybe it's time to create an oasis, to rediscover the purpose and blessing of a Sabbath. We're going to have to do this intentionally, consciously—create a space for our spiritual renewal.

I admit I'd rather be busy than bored, but I had an experience with my little great-nephew Cole that helped me more than he'll ever realize. I got to hold him and rock him to sleep, and then to just sit and watch him. I began to relax as I hadn't done in ages. I could feel it physically, emotionally, and even spiritually. It was like someone had hit the "dump the garbage" button on my overloaded mind, and I had an extraordinary, all-too-rare hour of sweet refreshment and renewal.

I've been thinking that maybe I shouldn't brag so much about never being bored. Maybe when a child says to you, "I'm bored," you should say, "Wonderful! I'll join you!" And you can sit or lie down and be bored together for a little while. What do you think? Maybe boredom is under-valued these days.

Can you think of how long it's been since you just sat and talked with your family—not in a movie or with the TV on or in the morning rush before everyone leaves for work or school, but just maybe in the evening or on a weekend or a Sabbath afternoon? Does that sound impossible? If we answer yes to that question, then there must be something wrong. No time to just sit and talk to each other? What has happened to us?

My friend Angie found out she had multiple sclerosis (MS) when she was very young. She began having symptoms even before she turned twenty. She reports one of her secrets to slowing down: "In my case, it wasn't by choice. Because I use a walker to walk with (or a wheelchair for long distances) I am forced to 'slow down and smell the flowers.' I have found that I am sometimes more observant of things and people around me."

Stephanie, who has become a well-known author, said she's becoming better at saying no to things she knows she can't do. (Let's get her to teach a class on the topic.) She says, "I try to limit myself to one function a week outside the home, whether an enrichment meeting, a class taught, or a whatever. I simply explain that I am the mother of three young children, and I am needed at home. Some do not understand, but others respond, 'Good for you.'"

One of my personal agonies is not being able to do all the "people things" I want to do. Elder Neal A. Maxwell wrote that he had a quote from Anne Morrow Lindbergh on his wall, and it's one of my favorites: "My life cannot implement in action the demands of all the people to whom my heart responds" ("Wisdom and Order," *Ensign,* June 1994, 41).

I've always loved it when my brothers have taken their children with them on business trips. What a fantastic idea. Maybe it makes it more difficult for them to get everything done, but maybe they're getting more important things done.

I've heard over and over, from many different sources: "Most people are doing exactly what they want to be doing." If that's true, then with prayerful consideration I'm convinced we can slow down enough not just to smell roses but to reconnect with our loved ones and ourselves and bring renewal and refreshment into our souls.

• *Don't skip or avoid leisure time.*

Arnold Toynbee reportedly said that "to be able to fill leisure intelligently is the last product of civilization."

In an excellent *Ensign* article some years ago, author Karen Lynn wrote about our tendency to let our "work ethic" overshadow other equally important aspects of life. Some of us actually fear leisure, she said, perhaps because "free time exposes our true interests; it reveals us for what we really are."

She went on to explain that guilt is born not of leisure, but of idleness. She then offered a helpful explanation of how the two are different: "Idleness puts us in a passive role, whereas leisure usually calls on us to participate mentally or physically or creatively; idleness merely passes time, whereas leisure fills personal needs; idleness occupies us, but leisure renews us; we put the responsibility for filling our idle time on something outside ourselves, whereas we look within ourselves for our leisure." ("'I Have Work Enough to Do' (Don't I?)," *Ensign*, August 1981, 42).

For those who know how to use their leisure time, it is really a gift. I love the days that I call "free days"—days, or even an hour or two, when I had something scheduled but it was cancelled.

• *See if you can consciously get along with less.*

Wanting less is probably a better blessing than having

more. It's a "heart condition," isn't it? With increased awareness and perspective, we can teach our hearts to be satisfied sooner, content with less.

• *Seek to know what Jesus would do, and then have the courage to do what you're prompted to do.*

As President Howard W. Hunter taught:

> Let us follow the Son of God in all ways and in all walks of life. Let us make him our exemplar and our guide. We should at every opportunity ask ourselves, "What would Jesus do?" and then be more courageous to act upon the answer. We must follow Christ, in the best sense of that word. We must be about his work as he was about his Father's. We should try to be like him, even as the Primary children, sing, 'Try, try, try' (*Children's Songbook*, p. 55). To the extent that our mortal powers permit, we should make every effort to become like Christ—the one perfect and sinless example this world has ever seen. ("What Manner of Men Ought Ye to Be?" *Ensign*, May 1994, 64)

That's all for now, folks. And no, you haven't just finished watching a cartoon. But those are some ideas about "What then shall we do?" Maybe you've thought of some ways to be more aware of the blessings that surround us, and some ways in which you might more fully enjoy, appreciate and share. Slow down. Do good and be good. Take time to rest, especially on the Sabbath. Take time for refreshment and renewal. Consider carefully the ideas the still, small voice has whispered to you.

The Law of the Fast and Consecration

Think back on some of your first experiences with fasting. Do you remember ever saying, "I'm starving!" or "I'm starved!" (Sometimes I'd even say things like that between meals, not just when I was fasting.)

When you were fasting, did you ever find ways to "cheat"? That's probably too strong a word, but did you ever sneak food into your room so you'd have something to help you survive? Did you ever watch the second hand on the clock for when the twenty-four hours would be up? Were there times when you ate so much to break your fast that you made up for anything you might have missed?

Do you remember when you first became aware of fast offerings? Do you remember when you first paid a fast offering yourself, or added to the family's contribution?

Now consider what consecration means to you—how

you would define or describe it—and then think of some ways in which you have worked to practice consecration in your life.

My first memories of fasting probably shouldn't be shared out loud, let alone be written down. Fasting was pretty much a "near-death" experience in those early days, a form of torture. I dreaded that first Sunday of each month, and the Saturday evening connected to it.

I knew I would be miserable, so I was. I anticipated a negative experience, so that's pretty much what I got. Oh, how I suffered! Why would God do this to us if He really did love us? I did not find one single thing to enjoy about it. Okay, maybe one single thing: We didn't have to wash as many dishes.

It was a while before I figured out *why* we fasted. Sometimes it was as if I was going on some "hunger strike" so that I could then "demand" something from God. I didn't give much thought to others, nor even to "Thy will be done." Maybe I thought that my fasting would change His mind!

Gradually I've changed *my* mind, and my heart, and my prayers, and so much else. All this is part of my process of learning. I've learned that there's a whole lot more to fasting than just a "Miss-A-Meal" experience and the paying of a little money.

We have been asked to be generous as we give, and not necessarily give only the amount saved from missing two meals. As President Spencer W. Kimball put it, "I think we should . . . give, instead of the amount saved by our two meals of fasting, perhaps much, much more—ten times more when we are in a position to do it" (*The Teachings of Spencer W. Kimball,* 146). The invitation is not that *everyone* should give ten times more, but that those who are in a position to do so can respond (see also Mosiah 4:26; Mosiah 18:27–29; and 2 Corinthians 8:12–15).

President Kimball also said that if we would give a generous fast offering, we would "increase our own prosperity both spiritually and temporally" ("Welfare Services: The Gospel in Action," *Ensign,* November 1977, 79).

Now, here's where I used to get caught up in the materialism and money thing all over again. Being blessed spiritually was something I would think about later, but the temporal part I was so excited about! Imagine—I increase my fast offering a little bit, and the financial, material, temporal blessings begin flowing in my direction.

Years ago I used to enter every sweepstakes I could find, hoping that I'd win $10 million or so. I'd actually start thinking of specific ways I would spend all that money. I'd list tithing first, just in case someone in Heaven was watching and listening, and my attitude would give me some extra help in being chosen as winner.

My friend Kathy shared the following, and I can relate so much to what she describes. She said she became aware that the California Lottery "pot" had grown to $100 million. When she heard that, she began thinking. (That's where it always starts with MEE too: the thinking . . . of all the things that could be accomplished with $100 million. In fact, I can hardly believe it when I read that lottery winners don't live happily ever after!)

So Kathy was thinking about all this money, and even though she had never in her life bought even one lottery ticket, this felt a bit tempting. She thought of good things she could do to help others. She got on a roll, as they say.

But the more she thought about all of this, the more she became aware that she wasn't allowing time to think of much else. Frustration set in, because she realized that the things she was daydreaming about weren't really possible. She recognized she may have been starting to covet what others had that she didn't.

And then she had a profound learning experience. As she described it to me, she realized that thinking about the lottery so much had made her *very* unhappy. She had not even purchased a single ticket, but even the *thinking* had made her discontent and upset. I think I get it.

This I'll tell you—the temporal blessings that have come to me as I've become more generous in my fast offering and other donations have been so unexpected (because I'm an earthling, thinking of money and "stuff and things") that I've almost missed them. Here's one of the major ones: I've become more aware of, thankful for, and content with what I already have. Isn't that incredible! I'm learning to be more satisfied, to have "enough" much sooner. This is a *process* rather than an *event,* I might add.

My perceptions about and feelings for the Law of the

Fast have changed so much as the years have gone by. It's almost as if I've had to take a lot of steps (not quite 12, but close):

1. Skipping a meal
2. Suffering
3. Skipping two meals
4. Suffering even more
5. Going without food and drink for twenty-four hours
6. Murmuring
7. Paying the equivalent of food I didn't eat
8. Being increasingly generous
9. Praying along with fasting
10. Fasting and praying with a purpose
11. Practicing "beginning consecration"

The Law of the Fast is a law of agency—I am free to fast whenever I want, whenever a prompting or need comes. Sometimes the Spirit will direct me to fast. I can have a private fast as well as joining with others—family, neighborhood, ward or branch, or the whole Church.

I am free to keep what I need of all that God shares with me, and then to share—*offer*—the rest. Striving to fully keep the Law of the Fast helps me to be increasingly free from selfishness and preoccupation with "stuff and things"—worldliness. Here is an opportunity to *voluntarily* go without food for not just physical but *spiritual* reasons. If sometimes my prayers need to be of better quality and more serious, I can fast along with praying.

Elder Joseph B. Wirthlin taught us:

> Those who choose to follow the example of the Savior and relieve suffering could look to the amount they contribute to fast offerings. These sacred funds are used for one purpose and one purpose only: to bless the sick, the suffering, and others in need.
>
> Contributing a generous fast offering blesses the givers richly and allows them to become partners with the Lord and the bishop in helping relieve suffering and fostering self-reliance. In our prosperous circumstances, perhaps we should evaluate our offerings and decide if we are as generous with the Lord as He is with us. ("Inspired Church Welfare," *Ensign*, May 1999, 78)

Little by little I'm beginning to see that doing our best to live the Law of the Fast is a way to qualify to return to the Savior and our Heavenly Father and feel comfortable with Them.

My favorite passage of scripture on the Law of the Fast comes from Isaiah:

> Is not this the fast that I have chosen? to loose the bands of wickedness, to undo the heavy burdens, and to let the oppressed go free, and that ye break every yoke?
>
> Is it not to deal thy bread to the hungry, and that thou bring the poor that are cast out to thy house? when thou seest the naked, that thou cover him; and that thou hide not thyself from thine own flesh?

Then shall thy light break forth as the morning, and thine health shall spring forth speedily: and thy righteousness shall go before thee; the glory of the Lord shall be thy rereward.

Then shalt thou call, and the Lord shall answer; thou shalt cry, and he shall say, Here I am. If thou take away from the midst of thee the yoke, the putting forth of the finger, and speaking vanity;

And if thou draw out thy soul to the hungry, and satisfy the afflicted soul; then shall thy light rise in obscurity, and thy darkness be as the noonday:

And the Lord shall guide thee continually, and satisfy thy soul in drought, and make fat thy bones: and thou shalt be like a watered garden, and like a spring of water, whose waters fail not. (Isaiah 58:6–11)

Oh, how I love these verses! They seem to connect so powerfully to Matthew 25:34–40, and to Mosiah 18:8–11 and 27–29, and so many other references. Could there be more tender and generous promises to us than to have our light break forth as the morning, to be able to call and have the Lord answer, to cry and to have Him respond with "Here I am"?

What would it be like if our darkness were as the noonday! How would our days be if the Lord were guiding us continually and satisfying our souls in drought. What if we could be like a watered garden and a spring of water whose waters fail not. Then no one would ever come to us thirsty—literally or figuratively—and find us without something to share to help take away that thirst.

Fasting is a commandment of the Lord. And so, as with all of Heavenly Father's commandments, there are wonderful, significant blessings attached. I guess it's not exactly that they're "attached"; they just come. They just happen when we're doing our best to keep commandments and covenants.

The Prophet Joseph Smith taught that "this is one great and important principle of fasts approved of the Lord. And so long as the saints will all live to this principle with glad hearts and cheerful countenances they will always have an abundance" (*History of the Church* 7:413).

Think of it—we will always have an abundance! We will always have "enough and to spare," or "enough and to share." Maybe it's as if Heavenly Father gives to us so that we can give to others. It's part of our practice in becoming more like He is. He is so *generous* with us, and He gives us the blessing of being generous with others.

Former Presiding Bishop Victor L. Brown has said that "when we give generously to the Lord, we receive from him that which is of greater value than our offering" ("A Vision of the Law of the Fast," *Ensign*, November 1977, 82). Has this been your experience?

As my dear friend Brother Lacanienta used to say when we would talk of such things in the Philippines, "The Lord is tricky." And he would describe how he would work to share pennies and minutes with those in need, and the Lord would *always* give them back, "with interest!"

The Law of the Fast has become a source of increased well-being and enjoyment for me as years and experiences have gone by. In the Doctrine and Covenants, fasting is tied to joy. Speaking of the Sabbath, the Lord said: "And on this day thou shalt do none other thing, only let thy food be prepared with singleness of heart that thy fasting may be perfect, or, in other words, that thy joy may be full. Verily, this is fasting and prayer, or in other words, rejoicing and prayer" (D&C 59:13–14).

Fasting is a way to express thanks and joy, a way to worship and praise God. When I realized that fasting had pretty much been made synonymous with rejoicing, it did away with my "near-death experience" kind of fasting.

How does the Law of the Fast help us with our consecration? It feels, again, like we are blessed with abundance and then we get to choose what we keep—"enough." And then we offer the rest, not just in fast offerings, but in other offerings as well (all the things listed on the donation slip, for example).

Read from Hebrews 13:5–6:

> Let your conversation be without covetousness; and be content with such things as ye have: for he hath said, I will never leave thee, nor forsake thee.

So that we may boldly say, The Lord is my helper, and I will not fear what man shall do unto me.

Now read verse 5 again, but this time the way Joseph Smith translated it: "Let your consecrations be without covetousness; and be content with giving such things as ye have; for he hath said, I will never leave thee, nor forsake thee."

Isn't that beautiful!

Elder Bruce R. McConkie taught powerfully of the connection between obedience, consecration, and sacrifice in a conference address:

> The law of sacrifice is a celestial law; so also is the law of consecration. Thus to gain that celestial reward which we so devoutly desire, we must be *able* to live these two laws.
>
> Sacrifice and consecration are inseparably intertwined. The law of consecration is that we consecrate our time, our talents, and our money and property to the cause of the Church: such are to be available to the extent they are needed to further the Lord's interests on earth.
>
> The law of sacrifice is that we are willing to sacrifice all that we have for the truth's sake— our character and reputation; our honor and applause; our good name among men; our houses, lands, and families: all things, even our very lives if need be. . . .
>
> What the scriptural account means is that to gain

celestial salvation we must be *able* to live these laws
to the full if we are called upon to do so. Implicit in
this is the reality that we must in fact live them to the
extent we are called upon so to do. . . .

And every member of his church has this prom-
ise: That if he remains true and faithful—obeying,
serving, consecrating, sacrificing, as required by the
gospel—he shall be repaid in eternity a thousandfold
and shall have eternal life. What more can we ask?
("Obedience, Consecration, and Sacrifice," *Ensign,*
May 1975, 50, 52)

Here's an idea for teaching these principles in a family
home evening activity or other setting. This idea is based
on a talk I heard years ago in stake conference. I don't
remember who gave the talk, or I would certainly give him
credit.

Prepare some collections of 10 things: 10 dimes, 10
pencils, 10 oranges, 10 packages of gum, and so on. Be creative, and gather groups of 10 things that will be of great
interest to those in your group.

You might want to begin with all of these things in a
sack. Everyone will be wondering what you have in the
sack. You don't show them right away. Instead, you express
thanks for all that Heavenly Father has shared so generously. Maybe you have a short discussion, asking those in
the family or group to name some of the things they've
noticed on that particular day.

Then, one by one, you bring the sets of items out of

the sack and offer one to each member of the group. And, as they take their dimes, their oranges, their pencils, or whatever, you ask, "Would it be all right if I asked you to give one back to me?" No problem, usually. Maybe you'll know the members of your group well enough to start with someone who will catch on and set an example. "Oh sure! Which one do you want?"

By the time you've done this with several of the items, it's likely most members of your group will have caught on, and you won't have even used the word *tithing*. It's a pretty dramatic way to point out that you get to keep nine things—He only asks that you give one back.

I've tried this to teach about other offerings, too. "Could you spare two oranges instead of just one?" The orange could be divided up, part of it going to fast offerings, part to build temples, part for missionary work, and so on. And you can help your family understand that sometimes in their lives they'll have a little more to share than at other times. It's up to them.

Invite your children to pray about tithing, fast offerings, and other aspects of your lesson and the gospel. Heavenly Father will answer their prayers. As they feel His Spirit help them to understand and believe, they will have their own deepening desire to be obedient, and they will be blessed abundantly. Teach them these things by example most of all.

At some point you might want to teach some "mysteries," such as the miracle by which nine pennies go further than ten, just as nine minutes go further than ten. When we do our best to be generous with all that does not belong to us anyway (because it belongs to God, who shared with us), He gives it back to us. May we be increasingly aware of this and all our other wonderful blessings!

Godliness with
Contentment

As you can tell, this is the last chapter in this little book. Oh how I hope you've enjoyed it, and that you've found some meaningful things to think about and do, perhaps some experiments with becoming more content.

I wish we could sit down together and talk about what you've been thinking and feeling as you've read and meditated. It has been such an important experience for me personally to gather and study and ponder all the information I could. I recognize, as I've said, that this book doesn't cover "everything." But you should have seen my first draft! It would have taken you years to read! I hope there's enough to give you some good ideas and some helpful information.

I wanted this particular title for the last chapter

because I love the phrase so much. And it seems nice to have all the other chapters "sandwiched" between the two that focus mostly on contentment.

The phrase "godliness with contentment" comes from the New Testament, from the writings of the Apostle Paul. It's hard not to include the whole chapter of 1 Timothy 6. Reluctantly I'm sharing only a few of the verses, but I encourage you to read and think about the entire chapter (verses 1–22) when you have a chance.

Here is what I've chosen to share, wanting to put "godliness with contentment" in context:

> If any man teach otherwise, and consent not to wholesome words, even the words of our Lord Jesus Christ, and to the doctrine which is according to godliness;
>
> He is proud, knowing nothing, but doting about questions and strifes of words, whereof cometh envy, strife, railings, evil surmisings,
>
> Perverse disputings of men of corrupt minds, and destitute of the truth, supposing that gain is godliness: from such withdraw thyself.
>
> But godliness with contentment is great gain.
>
> For we brought nothing into this world, and it is certain we can carry nothing out.
>
> And having food and raiment let us be therewith content. (1 Timothy 6:3–8)

Good counsel for us, isn't it? I want to share wholesome words in my communication with others—the words of the Savior. I want to provide, both by example and by what I share, an invitation to move toward being more Godlike and Christlike.

I don't want to let pride get in the way. I don't want to get caught up in quarreling and contention, in envy or jumping to conclusions. I don't want to get off the path and suppose that gain—getting more, having more, possessing more, being caught up in materialism and ever-increasing consuming—is godliness.

Oh, to realize that godliness with contentment is great gain! To become that way, to live that way . . . can we even imagine it? I don't know that I can, but the more I think about it and try to figure it out, the better it sounds and feels.

It's a good reminder, isn't it, that we brought nothing (no "thing") into this world, and that we certainly will not be carrying our stuff and things out when it's time for us to leave. And I love the sweet invitation from Paul to be content with what we have—enough food, enough to wear, and adequate shelter.

There's another title I was thinking about for this last chapter: "A Slow Day in the Fast Lane." Maybe I'll use that another time on another project, because I really like it. It brings to the mind an oasis—a fertile spot in the desert. Maybe that's what contentment is—and increasingly so in a life well lived—a break from the routine, from the busyness, from the fast-lane living that many of us experience day after day.

I want to ask a question that may have come to your mind as you read. It is a question I've asked more than a few times in my wanderings and ponderings: Is there anything wrong in having an abundance and living the good life? Is it wrong to have nice things, a beautiful home, a brand-new car, enough and to spare?

Certainly not, based on what we learn from the scriptures. Often in the scriptures the people are described as being exceedingly rich! It seems it was the people's *attitude* toward what they had (and didn't have) that got them into difficulties.

President Gordon B. Hinckley pointed this out in an article about covetousness.

> Yet none of us ever has enough—at least that is what we think. No matter our financial circumstances, we want to improve them. This, too, is good if it is not carried to an extreme. I am satisfied that the Father of us all does not wish His children to walk in poverty. He wants them to have comforts and some of the good things of the earth. In the Old Testament, He speaks of "a land flowing with milk and honey," of the fatlings of the flock, and of other things which indicate that He would have His children properly fed and clothed and sheltered, enjoying the comforts that come of the earth, but not to excess.
>
> It is when greed takes over, when we covet that

which others have, that our affliction begins. And it can be a very sore and painful affliction. . . .

I repeat that I wish everyone might have some of the good things of life, but I hope our desire will not come of covetousness, which is an evil and gnawing disease. I think of many of our younger single and married members; I hope that you will be modest in your physical wants. You do not need everything that you might wish. And the very struggle of your younger years will bring a sweetness and security to your later life. ("Thou Shalt Not Covet," *Ensign*, March 1990, 4)

In Doctrine and Covenants 59:16–21, the Lord promises so much if we will be obedient cheerfully and thankfully. Let's read the verses:

Verily I say, that inasmuch as ye do this, the fulness of the earth is yours, the beasts of the field and the fowls of the air, and that which climbeth upon the trees and walketh upon the earth;

Yea, and the herb, and the good things which come of the earth, whether for food or for raiment, or for houses, or for barns, or for orchards, or for gardens, or for vineyards;

Yea, all things which come of the earth, in the season thereof, are made for the benefit and the use of man, both to please the eye and to gladden the heart;

Yea, for food and for raiment, for taste and for smell, to strengthen the body and to enliven the soul.

And it pleaseth God that he hath given all these things unto man; for unto this end were they made to be used, with judgment, not to excess, neither by extortion.

And in nothing doth man offend God, or against none is his wrath kindled, save those who confess not his hand in all things, and obey not his commandments.

The fulness of the earth, and all the beasts and herbs and good things to wear, to eat, to observe, to enjoy. It pleases God to give us all these wonderful blessings. He wants them to be for our benefit, and he wants them to be nice to look at, and to make our hearts glad. And He wants us to remember to be thankful and obedient.

Obedience can bring unusual blessings. My friend Joy Evans, who served a mission in Tennessee with her husband, Dave, told of a family in their little branch who were fixing up an old home. They put their food storage in the attic. They had a daughter, age twelve, who slept below the attic. The rest of them were apparently on a lower floor. One night a fire started. The young girl heard popcorn popping, then bottles breaking. She realized there was a fire and awakened everyone. Although all their belongings were lost in the fire, all their lives were saved. Food storage saved them.

Here are some insights from Elder Dean L. Larsen on the blessings we receive as we keep the commandments:

> It has seemed that one of the inevitable side effects that occurs as people apply gospel principles in their lives is that their material circumstances also improve. This does not suggest that it should be the right nor the expectation of all who accept the gospel of Jesus Christ to become wealthy in the possession of the world's goods. The Lord has made it clear, however, that when his people are obedient, he desires to bless them with the necessities and the comforts of life so that none should live in want. . . .
>
> Historically, the abundance with which the Lord has blessed his people has proved to be one of their greatest tests. The cycles of their acquiring worldly wealth and their subsequent spiritual decline are well documented in scriptural and historical records. ("'Beware Lest Thou Forget the Lord,'" *Ensign*, May 1991, 10)

I've thought about what other ingredients there are for experiencing contentment. There is one I've saved until here in the last chapter. It's right up in the top few most important ingredients, critical to our salvation as well as our contentment. It is the ingredient called forgiveness.

In my experience, including my observations of others, the ability to forgive seems to bring a great sense of relief and joy along with peace and contentment. This is true both when we are forgiven and when we are able to forgive.

I've read the parable in Matthew 18:23–35 several times recently, trying to take it very personally. This is the parable of the servant who was forgiven a tremendous debt, only to find a fellowservant who owed him "pennies," and who begged for mercy just as he, the forgiven servant, had received. But the servant would not follow the example of the one who had just forgiven him, and had the other thrown into prison.

When the master who had forgiven the servant found this out, he expressed great disappointment.

> Then his lord, after that he had called him, said unto him, O thou wicked servant, I forgave thee all that debt, because thou desiredst me:
> Shouldest not thou also have had compassion on thy fellowservant, even as I had pity on thee?
> And his lord was wroth, and delivered him to the tormentors, till he should pay all that was due unto him.
> So likewise shall my heavenly Father do also unto you, if ye from your hearts forgive not every one his brother their trespasses. (Matthew 18:32–35)

This is an example to us, because through the atonement of Jesus Christ, generous forgiveness and mercy have been made available to us. If the Savior asked His Father to forgive those who crucified Him, do you think He will ask His Father to forgive us—forgive you, and forgive me?

He said that the soldiers knew not what they were doing; sometimes that's true with us as well. We do things that hurt others, even when it's unintentional.

More than thirty years ago I had an experience where I caused a great deal of pain and anguish to others. I felt horrible along with them, but I was also burdened because I felt I was the cause, however innocently, of what had happened. I had sought counsel from many whom I trusted, but nevertheless I was the reason for the suffering of so many, including myself. I no longer remember all the details of the experience, which is probably good, but I still wonder if others knew how deeply sorry I was, and how much I needed their forgiveness.

I include this experience, even without details, because I've been thinking about the need we sometimes have to hear those words: "I forgive you." And we need to say those words: "I forgive you." We may have gone through some process of letting go of anger or pain, and we feel we've forgiven someone, but we've never *told* them. And there are likely many times when we haven't forgiven *ourselves*.

My pondering about forgiveness has given me a deep sense of gratitude that there is such a thing—a chance to forgive, and a chance to be forgiven. Because of the Atonement, peace can come to our hearts, our homes, our relationships, our souls. As we forgive, we're doing what God wants us to do. He wants us to be compassionate and understanding with others and with ourselves.

One of the things I regret, which is painful even to remember although lots of years have gone by, happened when I was about thirteen and my sister Susan was about seven. I had gone to Las Vegas for my regular every-three-weeks visit to the orthodontist, and returned to our home in Cedar City to find that Susan had used my crayons.

I was pretty fussy about my crayons. I *loved* them when they were brand new. I used them carefully, not wanting to break them or rip the paper wrappers haphazardly. (There's got to be at least one reader out there wondering why someone age thirteen was still using crayons . . . just remember that we didn't have TV, okay?)

Susan hadn't asked me if she could use my crayons, and she damaged some of them. I don't remember what I said or did, but I know I wasn't kind. As we sometimes say, I let her have it!

What I didn't know until later was that she got some money out of her piggy bank and walked downtown and bought me another box of crayons. . . . And it was wintertime and very cold. I remember that there was a lot of snow on the ground.

When I found the new box of crayons, I cried. Here I am, fifty-plus years later, crying again even as I'm writing about it. I don't remember what I said to her then, but I hope I apologized and asked for her forgiveness. I need to ask her if she remembers this incident from so many years ago. I've thought I might buy her a box of crayons now, just to say I'm sorry again.

Can you think of some things you regret? Maybe my example seems not too huge or serious, but as you think about it, do you know what I'm trying to explain? Think of your life, and see if something or someone comes to your mind. It seems regrets are tied to the need for forgiveness—both to receive it and to give it.

It's all a miracle, really. This is especially true when I think of forgiveness in connection with our baptismal covenant—our opportunity to bear one another's burdens that they may be light. Think of the burden lifted from *both* us and others when we forgive! What a gift! What an un-worldly thing to do!

The "natural man" wants to get even, to punish, to feel what is termed "sweet revenge" (what on earth could be sweet in revenge?), to make sure justice is done. Forgiving lets go of all this, and thus really does lighten *our* burdens (there's not so much to keep track of and fuss about) as well as the burdens of others. We let Heaven decide how to sort things out.

It may be that the act of forgiving, with all our hearts (see Matthew 18:35 again), is a heart-changing experience. A healing experience. Sometimes it may be a process, too, and not just an event.

I love the way President Hinckley taught this:

> My brothers and sisters, let us bind up the wounds—oh, the many wounds that have been caused by cutting words, by stubbornly cultivated grievances, by scheming plans to "get even" with

those who may have wronged us. We all have a little of this spirit of revenge in us. Fortunately, we all have the power to rise above it, if we will "clothe [ourselves] with the bond of charity, as with a mantle, which is the bond of perfectness and peace." (D&C 88:125.)

"To err is human, to forgive divine." (Alexander Pope, *An Essay on Criticism,* 2:1711.) There is no peace in reflecting on the pain of old wounds. There is peace only in repentance and forgiveness. This is the sweet peace of the Christ, who said, "blessed are the peacemakers: for they shall be called the children of God." (Matt. 5:9.) ("Of You It Is Required to Forgive," *Ensign,* June 1991, 5)

See if you can think of someone who needs and wants so much to be forgiven. Ask God to help you do it—to forgive, to let go. Don't attach any strings or conditions—just let go. At some point perhaps your heart will allow you to say something like, "Please forgive me for not forgiving you. I'm so sorry. I forgive *you,* and I ask you to forgive *me.*"

Consider these two important scriptures: "I, the Lord, will forgive whom I will forgive, but of you it is required to forgive all men" (D&C 64:10). "Blessed are the merciful, for they shall obtain mercy" (3 Nephi 12:7).

We'll find what we're searching for. We'll be drawn to what we really want. As the Lord explained, "for intelligence cleaveth unto intelligence; wisdom receiveth wisdom; truth embraceth truth; virtue loveth virtue; light cleaveth unto light; mercy hath compassion on mercy and claimeth her own" (D&C 88:40).

The more we strive to deny ourselves of *all* ungodliness, the more we'll be drawn to that which is more godly—the more we *will* experience "godliness with contentment."

I grew up with parents who came from what we call humble circumstances. Dad used to tell of a Christmas when they had one orange, and they shared it so that each could have a little piece. Mom tells of a time when her mother, who was pregnant, wanted so much to have a little bottle of root beer, but it cost a nickel, and they didn't have a nickel. Things like that bring tears, and I wish I could have been there to give my grandmother a nickel.

My parents lived through the experience of the Great Depression, and that had a significant impact on them and whole lot of other people in that generation. They learned to work hard and to be frugal, and they endeavored to pass these and other values on to us children. Do you suppose there is anything in my parents' background that would give a clue as to why one of their daughters would save so many cardboard boxes? Maybe not.

Were my parents perfect? Of course not. Was our family "ideal"? No! Maybe I too often make it sound like everything was practically perfect when I speak or write about us, but we were and are normal.

My parents became two of the most content people I've

ever known. Pictures come into my mind, such as Mom out in the barn milking her cow or cows (sometimes two, mostly just one). She would play music on the radio and later send letters to tell the station which type of music and which specific songs the cows liked best.

I used to love sitting with Dad in the evenings when he had his bread and milk, sometimes with a piece of cheese. I also picture Dad sitting in his chair in the living room, reading the scriptures or working on crossword puzzles.

One thing I love so much is when our family gathers. We used to do that every week for Sunday dinner. I loved the visiting, the remembering.

Thanksgiving was such an amazing time for us. We'd sit down at the table, almost always with at least twenty family members and friends, and Mom would announce that the only thing she hadn't made or raised was the cranberry sauce.

She was really the epitome of self-reliance and generosity. For years she raised, killed, cleaned, cooked, and let us help eat turkeys and chickens. I remember the bathtub being filled with water, chunks of ice, and a whole bunch of turkey bodies, or chicken bodies, waiting for the next step in the long, hard process. Many of us chose *not* to bathe in that particular bathtub. And, oh yes, we got to help with more than just eating.

Mom and Dad would frequently say to us children that "We have all we need. Our wants are simple."

When it was time for my Daddy to go Home, I learned much more from him even in that tender process. He was 95, hoping to make it to 100. But his body began to slow down even though his mind and spirit never did.

The Christmas of 1997 was wonderful, because our Daddy was home with us. We had found a "pocket talker" so that he could hear us, and we really celebrated, taking turns talking to him, singing to him, sharing stories, reading something we had found. It was so sweet to be together.

And then, three days later, it was time for him to leave, to go Home. Everything that mattered most to Dad went with him, except for us, but we're sealed to him and will be with him forever if we're as good as we can be.

For his burial, he asked for a plain pine box with one rose on the top, and we honored his request. He said in things he wrote that he felt there was too much competition and debt in what happened in connection with funerals and burials.

He also didn't want anyone to spend a lot of money for flowers for him. So John suggested the last line of his obituary, which we know is exactly what Dad would have wanted: "Please, in lieu of flowers, take your family to dinner."

Dad was buried with several items, including one of his stethoscopes. He had become so good at listening to hearts, both literally and figuratively.

My mother turned ninety while I was writing this book. She can feel that she's slowing down, but she's still sharp, bright, funny, and makes some of the best choco-lates you could find anywhere.

In August of 2002, Mom had some surgery on one of her eyes, and through several unexpected miracles (there are no coincidences) she ended up living with my brother John, his wife, Melanie, their five children, and their pug dog, Ivan. She has been there since, and is happy and content.

President Spencer W. Kimball taught that "Peace, joy, satisfaction, happiness, growth, contentment—all come with the righteous living of the commandments of God. The one who delights in all of the worldly luxuries of today, at the expense of spirituality, is living but for the moment. His day is coming. Retribution is sure" (*Faith Precedes the Miracle*, 223–24).

My parents fit the category of those who are blessed—they have experienced peace, joy, satisfaction, happiness, growth, and contentment because of their devotion to living righteous lives.

Our Heavenly Father wants us to be happy, not miser-able, and He has shown us over and over again how much He loves to bless us. And He loves it when we bless and watch over each other, moving toward a time when He can once again call us Zion.

President Spencer W. Kimball taught of the ideal of Zion and some of the challenges to achieving such a way of living.

> Zion can be built up only among those who are
> the pure in heart—not a people torn by covetousness

or greed, but a pure and selfless people, not a people who are pure in appearance, rather a people who are pure in heart. Zion is to be in the world and not of the world, not dulled by a sense of carnal security, nor paralyzed by materialism. No, Zion is not things of the lower, but of the higher order, things that exalt the mind and sanctify the heart. . . .

As important as it is to have this vision in mind, defining and describing Zion will not bring it about. That can only be done through consistent and concerted daily effort by every single member of the Church. No matter what the cost in toil or sacrifice, we must "do it." That is one of my favorite phrases: "Do It." ("Becoming the Pure in Heart," *Ensign*, March 1985, 4–5)

One account of a group of people who achieved this is recorded in *The Pearl of Great Price*. It's the account of the people of Enoch. They became so good that in Moses 7:18 we read: "And the Lord called his people ZION, because they were of one heart and one mind, and dwelt in righteousness; and there was no poor among them." It takes Zion people to build a Zion society.

This particular society—this City of Enoch—will be coming back one day. Whenever you see a rainbow, in addition to thinking briefly of a pot of gold, think of the City of Enoch.

And the [rain]bow shall be in the cloud; and I will look upon it, that I may remember the everlasting covenant, which I made unto thy father Enoch; that, when men should keep all my commandments, Zion should again come on the earth, the city of Enoch which I have caught up unto myself.

And this is mine everlasting covenant, that when thy posterity shall embrace the truth, and look upward, then shall Zion look downward, and all the heavens shall shake with gladness, and the earth shall tremble with joy. (JST, Genesis 9:21–22)

Wouldn't it be amazing if we could embrace the truth such that we could be among those who look upward and join in the gladness and joy! I think you'll be there. I do.

I've prayed *much* as I've worked on this book, and one of the strongest impressions that has come into my heart is the feeling that each of you deserves to hear an honest "thank you." Why? Because you're so wonderful, that's why.

Thank you for your goodness, your generous hearts, your provident lives, your saintly kindness to others. I'm aware of so many who are on this same soul-searching journey, and I've learned so much from reading, studying, and observing. I thank them—you—for such important examples. Let's keep working on our quest for contentment, not letting anyone shout down at us from a high tower and make us feel guilty or wickedly opulent in the way we're living. We know we're working at doing better and being better, so let's not get discouraged or over-whelmed in the sometimes challenging process.

I've tried to include enough quotes from Church leaders and others that we can find good things to ponder and find ideas and a sense of direction in. And I have tried to include information from others in a context—not just choosing isolated quotes. I think that's one reason I decided to have an Appendix—so that you can go to articles or books and put my quotes in a bigger context (and perhaps come to some different conclusions than I did).

President Gordon B. Hinckley will have the last quote: "If we will live the gospel, if we will put our trust in God, our Eternal Father, if we will do what we are asked to do as members of The Church of Jesus Christ of Latter-day Saints, we will be the happiest and most blessed people on the face of the earth" ("Excerpts from Recent Addresses of President Gordon B. Hinckley," *Ensign*, April 1996, 72).

Let's do it!

It is my earnest desire that those who take the time to read this book will come across a few gems—an idea or a thought that will make a difference in a positive, happify-ing, contentifying direction. This chapter feels like the moment in the opera or the play when there's a "reprise" of all the themes throughout the whole production. I'm going to finish by borrowing and changing just a bit a famous expression: May contentment be with you this day and forever.

APPENDIX

A "Starter List" for Further Study

This is certainly not meant to be an exhaustive (or exhausting!) list of every single important thing that has ever been published on the subject of contentment and related topics. It is a list of some of the most enriching and thought-provoking articles I've found as I've been working on this book, and I know each reader will add more (and I'd love to know about them).

So I'm going to call this a "Starter List." It's only the beginning. As you find your own meaningful scriptures, books, articles, talks, quotes, and all, you can begin your own list, or just add to this one that I've started for you. You might even cross some of these off, finding that they aren't particularly helpful or interesting to you. That's all right too.

One thing I've discovered is that there are tons of resources on the internet about simplifying, handling money wisely, what do with and about material possessions, and so on. This really *is* just a "starter list." Have fun adding your own resources to the list!

ARTICLES

Benson, Ezra Taft. "'Pay Thy Debt, and Live.'" *Ensign,* June 1987, 3–5.

———. "Beware of Pride." *Ensign,* May 1989, 4–7.

Bradford, William R. "Unclutter Your Life." *Ensign,* May 1992, 27–29.

Christensen, Joe J. "Greed, Selfishness, and Overindulgence." *Ensign,* May 1999, 9–11.

Clapp, Rodney. "Why the Devil Takes Visa: A Christian response to the triumph of consumerism." *Christianity Today,* October 7, 1996, 19–33.

Daines, Robert H. "Making It to the Top: When Is the Price Too High?" *Ensign,* January 1985, 46–49.

Gardner, R. Quinn. "Becoming a Zion Society: Six Principles." *Ensign,* February 1979, 31–35.

Goode, Stephen. "Kilbourne Sees Beyond Advertising Pitch." *Insight,* May 15, 2000, 34–38.

Hinckley, Gordon B. "'Thou Shalt Not Covet.'" *Ensign,* March 1990, 2–6.

———. "To the Boys and to the Men." *Ensign,* November 1998, 51–54.

Howard, F. Burton. "Overcoming the World." *Ensign,* September 1996, 9–15.

Kindred, Sheila. "God's Treasures." *Friend,* April 1995, 27–29.

Largey, Dennis. "Refusing to Worship Today's Graven Images." *Ensign,* February 1994, 9–13.

Larsen, Dean L. "'Beware Lest Thou Forget the Lord.'" *Ensign,* May 1991, 10–12.

Lynn, Karen. "'I Have Work Enough to Do' (Don't I?)" *Ensign,* August 1981, 40–43.

Maxwell, Neal A. "Content with the Things Allotted unto Us." *Ensign,* May 2000, 72–74.

———. "The Prohibitive Costs of a Value-free Society." *Ensign,* October 1978, 52–55.

———. " 'Repent of [Our] Selfishness' (D&C 56:8)." *Ensign,* May 1999, 23–25.

———. "'Swallowed Up in the Will of the Father.'" *Ensign*, November 1995, 22–24.

McConkie, Bruce R. "Obedience, Consecration, and Sacrifice." *Ensign*, May 1975, 50–52.

Morrison, Alexander B. "A Caring Community: Goodness in Action." *Ensign*, February 1999, 13–19.

Nash, Scott. "Understanding Interest on Debt." *Ensign*, September 1997, 64–66.

Oaks, Dallin H. "'The Great Plan of Happiness,'" *Ensign*, November 1993, 72–75.

———. "Spirituality," *Ensign*, November 1985, 61–63.

Pace, Glenn L. "Infinite Needs and Finite Resources." *Ensign*, June 1993, 50–55.

"The Power of No (How to say 'NO' to your kids)," *Newsweek*, September 13, 2004, 42–51.

Romney, Marion G. "The Celestial Nature of Self-reliance." *Ensign*, November 1982, 91–93.

———. "Let Us Set in Order Our Own Houses." *Ensign*, January 1985, 3–6.

Sill, Sterling W. "A Fortune to Share," *Ensign*, January 1974, 60–62.

Tanner, N. Eldon. "Constancy amid Change." *Ensign*, June 1982, 2–7.

Top, Brent L. "'Thou Shalt Not Covet.'" *Ensign*, December 1994, 22–26.

Tucker, Larry A. "What's on TV Tonight?" *Ensign*, February 1988, 18–21.

Wirthlin, Joseph B. "Earthly Debts, Heavenly Debts," *Ensign*, May 2004, 40–43.

———. "Inspired Church Welfare." *Ensign*, May 1999, 76–79.

———. "The Straight and Narrow Way." *Ensign*, November 1990, 64–66.

———. "Windows of Light and Truth." *Ensign*, November 1995, 75–78.

BOOKS

Buck, Pearl S. *The Good Earth*. New York: Washington Square Press, 2004.

Chatzky, Jean. *You Don't Have to Be Rich: Comfort, Happiness, and Financial Security on Your Own Terms.* New York: Penguin Books, 2003.

Condie, Spencer J. *In Perfect Balance.* Salt Lake City: Bookcraft, 1993.

Frankl, Viktor E. *Man's Search for Meaning: An Introduction to Logotherapy.* New York: Pocket Books, 1963.

Hymns. Salt Lake City: The Church of Jesus Christ of Latter-day Saints, 1985. (Watch for those that emphasize the principles we've been sharing in this book.)

Kushner, Rabbi Harold. *When All You've Ever Wanted Isn't Enough: The Search for a Life That Matters.* New York: Fireside Books, 2002.

Oaks, Dallin H. *Pure in Heart.* Salt Lake City: Bookcraft, 1988.

Trapp, Maria Augusta. *The Story of the Trapp Family Singers.* Image Books, 1957.

MISCELLANEOUS

PBS programs, such as *Living Essentials,* that provide information on resource management (budgeting, saving, investing, and so on).

PBS program: *Affluenza.* The program is described as follows:

Af-flu-en-za *n.* 1. The bloated, sluggish and unfulfilled feeling that results from efforts to keep up with the Joneses. 2. An epidemic of stress, overwork, waste and indebtedness caused by dogged pursuit of the American Dream. 3. An unsustainable addiction to economic growth. 4. A television program that could change your life. (A production of KCTS/Seattle and Oregon Public Broadcasting made possible by a grant from The Pew Charitable Trusts. Host: Scott Simon.)

The writings of Hugh Nibley, especially "What Is Zion? A Distant View."

The writings of Gandhi, Mother Teresa, and Helen Keller.

For most "official" meanings of words I have used in this book: *The New Shorter Oxford English Dictionary.* Oxford: Clarendon Press, 1993.

Index

Index

Index

Index